SINGLE

SMART

C. KELLY HOWARD

CALICO PUBLISHING

Third Printing 1994
ISBN #: 0-9626232-0-2

For Information Contact:

CALICO PUBLISHING
P.O. BOX 276
SEABROOK, TX. 77586
U.S.A.
(713) 335-1608

Cover Design: Jeff Sensat
Sensat Creative Services

Look at what you have written. Does anything surprise you? Is it different than you would have thought? The same? Pick out the qualities you consider the most important. These are the real aspirations you have for the person you want to be with.

If you have trouble thinking of qualities, consider two or three of the people you admire. What draws you to them? What about them do you admire? These probably are similar to what you would like to find in other people in your life, such as a partner or a friend.

The better we know ourselves, the easier it is to know what we really want. Introspectively we realize, as individuals, that we are the only person who can truly decide what is right for us. What we want, do not want, like, or do not like is our final decision. One of the methods we can use to determine what our goals are is to understand where we are now, where we are going, and how we plan to live our life on our way there.

Where are you going in life? What are your long-range goals, wants, and desires? If you wish to live in Vermont on a farm with your husband and a large family, you would hardly justify a long-term relationship with an international businessman whose nights are spent socializing in expensive restaurants. Initially, you might be drawn to this man. He might be very exciting. However, you should understand that a long-term relationship with this person would not satisfy your goals. Relax and accept this relationship for what it is. Where are you presently in your life? Where you are now affects how and when you acquire something that you desire. Are you ready to settle down or have you just recovered from a divorce and would like to "date around"? Are you looking for adventure or safety? Have you already raised a family, or is that ahead of you? Are you set in your career or embarking on something new? Take into consideration your stance on relationships, marriage, children, your job or career, where you want to live, your long-term philosophies, your spiritual views...

How do you live your life? What is your lifestyle? Are you a "party animal" or a social recluse? Does money matter, and do appearances count? Do you like dining out and being seen or watching movies at home?

What do you expect out of life? Do you expect the absolute best that life has to offer, or are you willing to settle for what life offers you? Are you somewhere in between?

Complete the following:

I expect life to treat me:

I expect to get ________ of what I want (most, some, little, a lot...).

Are you satisfied with what you expect out of life?

How would you change this?

What are your values? What is the essence of your inner core? (Core values are your basic beliefs about right and wrong, good and bad.) List your values in the following space. Examples might be: Lying is wrong, stealing is wrong, you should always be courteous to your elders, religious freedom is important...

Nancy had decided she was ready to share her life with someone. Not just anyone. She wanted a very special person. She met someone who appeared to share a portion of her dreams and goals. It progressed and developed into a relationship. She found herself continually overlooking the way he treated other people. Although he was always courteous to her, he continually treated others rudely. She mentioned this to him, and his reply was that these people were unimportant so there was no reason to waste a smile on them. She began to realize one of her most basic beliefs was that you should always treat others as you would like to be treated yourself. To be able to see each person as an individual with feelings and a life of his own was very important to her. She made the decision that she would be unable to spend the rest of her life with someone whose beliefs were so different from hers. Since she knew what she wanted in life, she was able to leave the relationship relatively painlessly. She is now married and ecstatic about her husband and their relationship. They share many basic values yet maintain their individuality.

It is time to address the goals for your life. In the following space, write down your goals and desires. These can be based on anything: family, appearance, relationships, money, living accommodations, career aspirations, etc. Again, write down the first things that come to mind and you can sort through them later. Continue to add to and evaluate this list.

My Ultimate Goals:

Goals and Actions to accomplish in the next six months:

The next eighteen months:

Three-to-five-year goals:

Long-term goals (five years or more):

Looking at your overall life plan will help you determine what is important and where your areas of focus should be. Goals encompass your achievements and often are stepping stones toward other goals. For example, take a person who wants her body in shape, muscular, and toned. She also wants to loose thirty pounds. The weight loss becomes a step toward the well-toned body, since it is virtually impossible to have a well-toned body carrying thirty extra pounds. Thus, the weight loss is a short-term goal while the toned body is a longer-term goal. Recall the beginning of this book. I described the steps I took to achieve my own ultimate relationship. I knew in that order to have a perfect relationship, I first had to divest myself of the negative. This becomes a short-term goal or a building block toward something much more grand.

Goals allow us to develop clarity of intent. This in turn allows us to focus energy where we need it and not in a haphazard fashion. Professional studies have been done on the reasons why some succeed while others do not. The general consensus is that successful people are those who know where they are going and take the appropriate actions to get there. You probably know some successful people. They may not appear smarter, better, or quicker, yet they have done something you consider successful. A person achieves success because of clarity of intent or, in other words, they knew what they wanted and kept at it until they produced the results. The world is filled with stories of people who have succeeded in their endeavors, usually against great odds. Over and over, you will see how that person knew what they wanted and kept at it. How can you make this work for you?

Decide on your ultimate goal. Address all pertinent areas. This should be the best you can see for yourself, something that seems far off but not completely impossible. For example: You are presently involved in a couple of nondescript relationships, but the ultimate goal you seek for yourself is your "perfect" relationship.

Write it down, and declare it. For example: "My ultimate relationship goal is to be in a relationship filled with love, compassion, intimacy, fun and support".

Assume your need will be filled. Assume and surround yourself with the attitude that your desire will come to you. There is no stopping you. If circumstances appear contrary to what you want, look around them for what you know will come to you.

Move into action by...

Looking at where you are presently. Do your present circumstances reflect where you want to be? Are you in dead-end relationships? Confront this dilemma! Decide to accept your "ultimate goal".

Deciding upon a course of action based on your personal circumstances. Each case is different. We are all individuals in different circumstances. So, evaluate where you are and go from there.

Chapter Summary

Decide what you want, before you look for it!

Look for qualities that are most important to you. Be willing to negotiate and what really isn't that important. Be realistic.

Remember to take into consideration:

Where you are going,

Where you are presently,

How you live your life,

What your values are.

Chapter Three: Your Masterpiece

The next step is to bring your ultimate partner to life. This is done by giving life to the qualities you desire. Use the example of outgoing. What is that in real life? It could be a person who likes people and smiles a lot. Or it could be someone who is comfortable starting conversations and who communicates well. What if we use the example of attractive: Think of all the attractive people you know or have met. Notice how each one was different from others, yet they were all attractive to you. Feel these qualities in your life, feel what they are like to be with, as if they are already with you. Think of all the different ways each of these qualities can be expressed.

EXERCISE:

What are activities you will share? What emotions do these evoke? List these in the following space. Sports, hobbies, and of anything you enjoy doing. It is time to be come more involved in your goals.

Examples:

Reading, Hiking, Sailing, Laughing, Talking...

To become fully involved with your decision, we will use a technique called treasure mapping or creating your masterpiece. This is locating pictures and words that describe what you want in your life. These pictures, words, and essences will depict what your relationship looks like to you. Collect your magazines and pictures and purchase a large piece of poster board. Search for words, illustrations, and sentiments that describe the relationship you want. Make the emotion and feeling around your masterpiece one of perfect love, peace, and joy. Include all aspects of your relationship: emotional, mental, spiritual, physical. Include activities you imagine doing together. Show lovers embracing and superimpose your picture on them. The masterpiece technique works by providing additional clarification, especially for your subconscious. Thus, you clear your mind of clutter and attract only your goals. Remember, it is important to visualize what you want. This will enable you to recognize it when it comes along.

You should keep your masterpiece private. This will assure that you are creating your exact life designs without catering to the opinion of others.

Chapter Summary

Create your masterpiece to invoke the emotions you want in your relationship.

This is your creation - Create exactly what you want!

Chapter Four: Cleaning up your life

Is it time for a relationship in your life that works? Look at yourself. Are you reflecting this in your life? Or...

> *Are you nursing old hurts instead of presenting a whole and complete you?*
>
> *Are you still mad at or in love with your ex-husband, your ex-wife, your old boyfriend, or the person who broke your heart?*
>
> *Are you holding onto a relationship that is easy?, one that you know deep down, no matter how you work at it, is not the best you can do?*

You may be afraid that if you let go, you may never find someone else. Or even worse, that person you have been holding on to may immediately go out and fall in love. Then where would you be?; not only alone but probably mad too! You must create room in your life for your goals. You are allowing room for something better to come to you. Before you buy new furniture or a new wardrobe you make room by divesting yourself of the old. It is the same with relationships. If you have been mourning the loss of a lover or still feel anger or guilt, there is no room for someone new in your life. Until you release the old, you can not make room for the new.

Leftovers are dead weight, a drain on your energy. Completion is about being personally satisfied with every outcome in your life. In some cases, it means staying with something until it is done. In other cases, it means ending an unrewarding situation. To complete something means you must be personally satisfied with the results and your feelings surrounding those results. Incompletions take away from present situations and use up energy. This recovered energy can be used to improve and expand your life.

Is there anyone or anything from the past that you need to release or finish with? Is there someone in your life you are still hanging onto, even though he is already gone? Is there someone you constantly bring up in conversations or stories, someone whom you still call or still calls you? Is there anyone whose name brings up strong emotions whenever mentioned or when you see her?

Complete the following with those questions in mind:

Write down whoever or whatever you have not finished with.

Ask yourself if you are ready to release them? Are you ready to get on with your life? Can you wish them the best so you may also go on and find your best?

When you feel you are ready, write each one a note of completion. In it include what you enjoyed and what you disliked and the mention that the relationship was not perfect but fine just the way it was. Even though you may have built it into something wonderful, in your minds we now see it for what it really was. Also, include lessons you learned. Thank them and love them unconditionally as they are. Set them free, and wish them well. You don't have to mail the letter, but be sure that everything you write is the truth and that you could mail it if you wanted to.

Examples:

Dear Donald,

Thank you for the times we shared together. I hated you for your indifference to my innocence, your running around, and your lies. I realize now that you taught me to really get to know someone before I throw myself into his life. I forgive you for everything I felt you did wrong and wish you the best of luck. I hope that life is good to you.

Dear Donna,

I am sorry that our relationship didn't work out the way we had planned. I know we had a lot of fun and good times, but deep down there were some basic elements missing. This was not your fault or mine it is just where we were at the time. I have learned a lot from our relationship. I learned that I personally needed to grow, needed to expand myself and my beliefs. I thank you so much for the fun and the love that we shared. I wish you the best and truly hope you find everything you want.

Use the following space to write your own completion letters:

When you have finished, be certain that you believe all that you have written. Then take several deep breaths and visualize that person that you have written to. Read the letter aloud to them. Thank them for listening, and then see them leaving, walking away free of any bonds to you. Know that both of you are happy, whole, and complete. Take several more deep breaths. We never lose anyone. The structure of our relationship may change but in our hearts we still have the memory of people we have loved.

This exercise can be used when someone will not let you go. Be certain that you communicate as clearly as possible your desires to them. Make sure you are not giving mixed signals. Then, you can take further action by completing the above exercise.

Also use this exercise for anyone you haven't forgiven in your life. Do you harbor anger at your parents for the way they raised you or things they did or didn't say? Who in your life haven't you forgiven? Your brothers or sisters? Best friends? Is there someone whom you felt hurt you and let you down?

Have you forgiven yourself? Take some time and write down everyone who comes to mind. Then write your notes of completion, and let the people go. Know that the past is gone and forgiveness releases you. You are free to go forward.

EXERCISE:

Look at anything left over in your life.

List every situation in your life that had an unsatisfying ending.

Continue to write the reasons for your dissatisfaction until you get to the truth.

Now ask yourself: what can I do to complete this to my satisfaction, forever?

Do whatever comes to mind.

Example 1:

I have never completed my French lessons. I am not satisfied with this because it is something I said I would do.

First, I ask myself, "Is this something that is still important to me?" My answer to myself is, "Not really." As much as I enjoy traveling, I find I am quite capable of getting by on my present knowledge of French. To complete this, I forgive myself for not finishing a task I started and just let it go.

Example 2:

Sheila did not like the way her termination was handled at a particular job. First, she listed the reasons for her dissatisfaction. Next, she asked herself if this is was a position (it could be a relationship) she still desired? She could truthfully answer "no". She is now able to explore new and perhaps better career opportunities. To complete this she listed every valuable asset and action her talents brought to that particular position. After realizing she was now in a much better position than before, she was able to let her concerns and resentments go. Use this space to complete any leftovers you may have in your life.

Look around at your own personal space: your room, your home, and your office. Do you keep memories of your past relationship around? Pictures taken together, special gifts, things that constantly remind you of someone you are trying to let go of. Do you have clothes you are keeping only because that person particularly liked you in those? Look through your stuff. What value is it to you? I am not proposing that you throw away all of your pictures and keepsakes. Just look at what you are keeping and ask yourself why? If it is because you don't want to give that person up, maybe you better look at these things again. Go on from here to clean up all of your space completely. Allow room in your life for what you want. Do not clutter it with leftovers.

You will be amazed at the energy and lift this small exercise will give you. Give these items away with a glad heart, thanking them for all of their service to you and send them on for someone else to enjoy and use. Make room in your life for new treasures.

Chapter Summary

Create room in your life for what you desire.

Leftovers are dead weight.

Completion is power in action.

Forgiveness releases you to go forward in your life.

Take a chance, and get rid of whatever is holding you back.

Chapter Five: Releasing The Present

Now, we will look at the relationships presently in your life. Often, people have casual love relationships in their life, even though they are looking for someone new or permanent. The mistaken belief is you can hang onto this person as a lifesaving device until someone throws you a new one. You must release the old ring before you can firmly grasp the new.

Jack had divorced two years before. However, he still felt guilty about it, as if he had betrayed his wife, Ann. Because of this, he continued to see her after the divorce, even though he knew she wanted nothing more than to get back together. He didn't want that, but it was comfortable because there were only a few of the pressures he found with other women and he was familiar in dealing with those. Jack and Ann never completed with each other. It became a habit to drag the relationship on.

Then Jack began dating Chris. The closer he became to Chris, the more threatened Ann felt and the more confused Jack became. Even though he said he was through with Ann, he had never let her go, so their relationship was infringing upon his new one. After several months Chris gave Jack an ultimatum. He would have to explain to Ann that their relationship was over and let her go, or Chris would leave. He found he was unable to overcome his guilt and walk away from his ex-wife. Shortly thereafter Chris left. Jack knows that his relationship with Ann is pointless, but he has not let himself complete with her. Since he is still caught in this treadmill, he is unable to go forward into a new relationship.

You know if you have a relationship like this in your life. It may be as complicated as someone you have left several times, yet you still go back. It may be as unrewarding as someone with whom you have sex whenever they call (or you call them), but there are no real feelings. These types of relationships are destructive because they take away from ourselves. We go along with them, telling ourselves we will leave when something better comes along. What we don't realize is that these relationships keep us from what we want, eliminating the room in our lives for someone special. We are unable to think or see clearly.

How do you know when a relationship in your life isn't working? If you are unsure and want to be certain, here are some questions you can ask yourself.

Do you tell the truth about how you are feeling?

Are you happy around your partner?

When your partner's name is mentioned do you smile and feel good or do you feel burdened and unhappy?

Do you feel twinges of anger or disillusionment around your partner?

Initially, you might think that anyone experiencing these negative emotions would leave. Think of two couples you know. Do they pass the simple questions on this test? Do they still like each other, respect each other, carry on lively conversations, praise more than complain about the other? If you can honestly say that all the couples you know could pass the compatibility test, then you are doing well. You are surrounding yourself with wonderful friends as role models of love. If, in fact, you thought about several couples and they didn't pass the test, chose one of the couples and answer these questions.

Is this state that they are in recent? How long have they actually been estranged? Months? Years? They are together, yet they couldn't pass a simple compatibility test. Would they be happier if they could change or leave the relationship?

Most likely they stay. They are afraid of letting their true emotions show, afraid to let the other person go, afraid their partner may find someone better and afraid they will be unable to replace them. On and on, yet it is really all the same — fear of the unknown. Most things in life are unknowns, but that shouldn't stop you from living.

Are you completely happy in all your relationships? Are you willing to do whatever it takes to make them right? Are you content to spend the rest of your life in lukewarm relationships, just getting by or in an easy relationship in which you don't have to give 100 percent? (Remember, as you give, so you receive.)

If you haven't given up your vision of a fun and fulfilling relationship, then you need to move past your lukewarm not-as-happy-as-you-could-be-should-be-relationship. This doesn't mean just your lover/partner relationship this means all of them! Do you have friends you play with not because you really want to but for lack of anything better to do? Do you have people in your life who you can't relate to, who you do not trust, and who get on your nerves? However, you are still with them because it's easier than trying to make new friends? Don't all of our relationships tell us something about our lives? Can we be a complete, happy, and harmonious couple and have unhappy friends? In the space below, write down ten relationships you have presently in your life. (your lover, mother, father, friends, co-workers, boss ...)

Under "yes" list the reasons to keep that person in your life.
Under "no" list the reasons you avoid that person.
Note the changes you would like to make.
Then commit to making them.
When all our relationships work, so does our life!

PERSON	YES	NO	CHANGES

How do you release relationships that aren't working? Do it honestly! The longer an uncomfortable situation exists, the more destructive and hurtful it becomes. You must face your relationships and say:

I'm sorry, but what I want from our relationship is:

but I feel I am getting:

It is time to change or let go. Release your insecurities. Once it is done and past, you'll wonder why you hadn't done it sooner!

Chapter Summary

Let go of the old before you expect something better to come to you. You have to make room!

Most of life is unknown. Don't freeze yourself in fear.

When our relationships work, so does our life!

Chapter Six: Patterns

When you take time to examine your life, do you notice that certain events seem to happen again and again? Does this happen in your relationships? Think back over the years, and note your relationships. Are there negative incidents that seem repetitive? For example, it could be that you pull back when you get close to someone. Do you get involved in a relationship to the exclusion of all of your friendships and then suddenly feel trapped and run? Your patterns of the past may be holding you back. Take some time to reflect on any negative patterns you may have in your life. In the following space, write any answers that come to mind.

Examples:

Pattern:
I always cause a fight when I get close to someone.

Why do I do this?
It pushes my partner away because I am afraid of intimacy, afraid of being close.

Pattern:
I always change girlfriends when I change jobs.

Why do I do this?
I am afraid of being judged for not being successful.

If you find a fear that you really believe, acknowledge it. Don't ignore it or belittle it. There is a reason that you have this fear. It may have protected you in the past. Try to see it for what it is, something you created for a reason. It has served a purpose. Decide if you need to continue keeping and embracing this fear. If you are ready to let it go, then do the following:

State the fear.

Example:

I am afraid of intimacy because I might get hurt.

Write a releasing statement, sign it and date it.
Some people like to burn it and let the ashes fall away (symbolic of releasing the old).

I (your name) am now ready and willing to release my fear of intimacy. I acknowledge that I am completely safe in my relationships.

Allow your new freedom by declaring it.

I (your name) now allow myself to experience intimacy and safety in my relationships. Thank you.

Write an affirmation about your new belief:

I (your name) experience only safe intimate relationships.

Knowing how and why you react is important if you are to go forward in a relationship. Realizing that you are reacting to a behavior pattern in your past allows you the opportunity to release it. This gives you the power to act instead of react in situations in which, at one time you would have just repeated the pattern. Many people are able to release old fears and immediately move into something more wonderful and energetic than they had thought possible. If you feel that letting go of old fears has opened a can of worms, relax. You may be trying too hard. Breathe deeply. Realize that the fear is probably unfounded. If you truly believe this, then circumstances will change for the better immediately. Remember, you maybe changing core beliefs. A little disruption means that something is really happening.

Chapter Summary

All fears serve a purpose, if yours no longer serve you, let them go.

Learning about yourself helps you understand your actions and reactions.

Chapter Seven: Parents

Many times people repeat the relationship they perceive their parents had, when it is improbable that they are actually aware of the contents of their parents' relationship. This is fairly normal and could be one of the factors in the growing divorce statistics. Divorce has become normal.

No one is condemned to live their parents' relationship. Even though that was your first role model, you have the power to choose another. Look to people who you know exemplify the relationship you desire. Model them. If it has already been done, then you know that you too can do it. If you feel stuck, seek outside help. Help can take the form of a group, a counselor or a friend. The shape it takes does not matter. Just find something that works.

How many couples do you know who started off with dreams and visions only to realize three, five, or twenty years later that they had grown so far apart that they barely knew each other. The partnership had definitely vanished. Maybe this happened to your parents, even if they did not divorce. Do your parents still lovingly share in each others lives? If so, congratulations. You have role models in your own home. Ask them what they attribute to their success.

If your own parents do not fit your idea of a perfect couple, then realize you grew up modeling something that you do not want. It could be that being a couple in name only is not what you want for the rest of your life. If being in love and being together is important to you, then you need to change what your ideas of relationships are. Whether you believe them or not, your ideas on how couples are supposed to interact came first from your family. Did you grow up in a single-parent home and now believe that you have to be on your own to make it in life? Did one of your parents travel all of the time, and you now believe that your partner will never be there for you? What was your parents relationship when you were growing up? Did they demonstrate their affection in front of you or is affection only for courting? Do you feel that public displays of affection are wrong? Did your parents tell you they loved each other but you never saw anything but distance between them? Do you now believe relationships should be at arm's length?

EXERCISES:
Answer the following questions to the best of your knowledge.

What was your parents' relationship like?

What would you like to have seen different?

What would you like to have seen kept the same?

How similar are your relationships to that of your parents?

What was growing up like?

What beliefs came from your family?

How did your parents treat each other?

What did your parents tell you about relationships?

What do you believe about what you saw or were told?

What did you learn that you want to keep?

Even if your parents' relationship is not the one you want in your life, acknowledge it for what it was. It was a powerful teaching tool in your life. Your parents' relationship may affect your relationship goals. Our parents did the best they could, given the circumstances of their lives. A good way to see how wonderful your parents are/were is to write down what you learned from them and their relationship. Positive, negative, or neutral. When you write it, you will begin to see how it has benefitted you. It has helped to make you the person you are today. Tell your parents, "Thank you!"

Positive:

Negative:

Neutral:

Chapter Summary

Divorce doesn't have to be normal.

Your parents were probably basing their relationship on the one their parents had! It is time to stop the patterns and have what you want.

If your parents didn't have a perfect relationship, it's okay to be different. They will be proud of you for breaking the mold.

Chapter Eight: Friends

Our friends play various roles in our lives. They can be sounding boards, providers of advice, playmates or role models. Friends influence the way we think and feel especially if we spend a lot of our time with them or respect what they have to say.

Do your friends support you in your endeavors? Let those who do support you know that you are taking complete responsibility for your life and relationships.

What are your friendships based upon? Is it mutual enjoyment or just gossip (especially around the opposite sex)? Are your friends comfortable with you when you are in a relationship or do they feel left out?

I recently traveled to a city where a single girlfriend of mine lives. I called to invite her to dinner. When I reached her, she said several of her girlfriends were going out for dinner and we would meet at the restaurant. What followed was interesting. We were five attractive single career women out for dinner. The entire evening was spent discussing two topics. The first was that there are no "good" men to date, and if there were, it would be impossible to find them. Also, if you did find one, he was married. The second topic of conversation centered on another friend who was not there. She was on a date. They talked about everything that was going wrong in her life and how this guy was probably as bad as the last one (even though no one had met either of the men).

I realize that I am making these women out to be shrews. They really are not. As friends and confidants though, they were reinforcing each other's negative beliefs.

There are no "good" men. If you do find a "good" man, you are being disloyal to your friends. This story is included so you may see what influence our friends have in our lives. Listen to your friends' conversation. Is it up-beat and positive or downtrodden and miserable?

You do not have to change your friendships; just become aware of their influence. Some of your friendships may change as you do.

Friends who believe that life doesn't get better will become uncomfortable around you as your life becomes more joyous and energetic. You will serve as a inspiration to some, and they will join you in your new lifestyle. Others will take longer. That is truly everyone's choice. Your choice is to be with friends who you feel happy and joyful around. To be with people who love and support you without prejudice or hypocrisy is a rewarding and empowering experience.

EXERCISE:

Look at your friends, and write down the names of your favorite friends and those who you spend the most time with.

Is their talk positive or negative?

Is their life moving forward or remaining stagnant?

Do they smile positively, or do they complain constantly?

What input do you get from your friends?

Do they support you, or do they undermine you?

You can create your friendships just as you want them to be. Be honest with your friends. Honesty is the crux of all relationships. Tell them how you feel, how they affect you and what you would like. Being honest and open with your friends is a great way to prepare yourself for honesty in a relationship.

Often, as people move into relationships, they tend to ignore or spend less time with their friends. Friendships can enhance your relationships. What were once exclusive friendships will become mutual friendships as your relationship develops. Do not view previous friendships as competition for your relationship. Instead of assuming this viewpoint, cultivate your partners' friends. If your partner has them as a friend, you will probably enjoy these new associations.

Chapter Summary

You can chose your friends so chose the ones who support you.

Your choice is to be with friends you feel happy and joyful around.

Honesty is the crux of all relationships. Practice with your friends!

Chapter Nine: Your Personal Profile

Another way of determining your goals is to discover who you are and what you like. A personal profile will help you. It is an overview of your big picture. You will uncover traits and wants you may have forgotten you had. At the same time you will see where you are and where you are going. Fill in the following form. Add additional information at the bottom in the space provided.

Name and any nicknames you have had.

Where do you live?

Where do you work, and what is your employment history?

Areas in which you have excelled in your life.

Nonwork - related positions you have held in your life.

Personal history; family, friends, pets...

Physical statistics.

Activities you enjoy.

Activities you don't enjoy.

Other areas of interest.

Personality traits you like about yourself and why.

Exciting things you have done in your life.

What magazines do you enjoy?

What causes do you support (or would like to)?

Traits you like/don't like in others.

What is your favorite vacation you have taken and why?

Where are you going in life?

Who will be there with you?

Things you would like to do.

Why haven't you done them?

Sports and activities you participated in, in grade school, high school, and college.

If you could have anyone for a friend, list three people you would like to know.

Resume's are autobiographies we use to convince people of our worth and knowledge. A personal profile is similar to a resume' in that it will help you to see your worth. Although I am not recommending that you hand yours out (especially en mass), that is how Jon finally persuaded me to give him the attention he deserved. After numerous attempts to ask me out, he asked in exasperation if I needed to see his resume' beforehand. The next time we met, he presented me with a personalized version of his resume'. I realized how lucky I was to meet someone this fun and imaginative. I had been avoiding accepting what I had asked the universe for.

Chapter Summary

The better you know yourself, the easier it is to know what you want.

Chapter Ten: Enjoying Your Own Company

Do you enjoy sitting home alone, possibly watching the third rerun of some sit-com? You don't? Why not?

Now you might be wondering if there is something wrong with the author. Isn't the whole point of this book to reduce time spent sitting home alone? Well, yes, but ... I am sure you have heard the saying, "How can you enjoy being with others until you learn how to enjoy being with yourself?"

Consider what that means. If you don't enjoy being by yourself, you will try to find others to "save" you. By doing this you are looking to someone else for your salvation. When they are gone, once again you are alone, and it is up to you and only you. The paradox is that the more comfortable you are by yourself, the more you will like and love yourself, and the more people will want to be with you.

Do you find that you accept any invitation that comes to you just to avoid being alone? How many dates have you accepted because you didn't want to sit at home again. Yet, after thirty minutes, boredom has set in like concrete, and you are wondering why you ever accepted the date! Think of the wasted time. You could have been doing something with yourself that you really enjoyed. You could have been working on something important to you or just being by yourself-pizza, grubby clothes, a wonderful dog (whose conversation is never boring), and a movie you love to watch.

Have you ever considered that you are the only person who can please yourself 100 percent of the time? Do you? If it is just you, there are (hopefully) no heated discussions about who has the remote control, whether you eat Chinese or Mexican, how obnoxious your loud music is, etc. Being one half of a whole couple is wonderful. Until you meet your other half, realize that right now you are the whole! There is just you. There may be friends, lovers, and acquaintances in your life, but you are the totality of your existence. Enjoy yourself. Celebrate you. See yourself for the wonderful person you are, and have fun by yourself. This will make you realize that people should and will want to be with you because you are great! Realize that, and suddenly you will be by others who want a little of your magic. You will then know you are ready to share yourself and be a contributing part of a whole relationship.

There is nothing wrong with wanting to be with other people. We are gregarious by nature. If you find yourself with people you don't want to be with or doing things you don't want to, you will begin to appreciate your own great company! Don't beat yourself up for getting stuck on a boring date. Just keep it in mind next time.

Give yourself permission to do what you want to do. Have fun. Having fun is the surest way to attract someone into your life. If responsibilities seem to hold you back, remember, you determine your responsibilities! Think back on a time in your life when responsibility had one vote and pleasure had two. Didn't you still take care of your responsibilities? Doing things you really like to do adds energy and creativity to your life.

Get rid of superficial relationships, especially the ones that drag you down and give you more time in discomfort than in joy. Release them, and let them go their own way. It may be tough at first but in the long run you will be much happier. If you are not comfortable with yourself then you won't be comfortable by yourself. If you do not take time to be by yourself, you will never learn what you are not comfortable with. Learn to enjoy the time you spend by yourself.

Exercises: Learning to love and enjoy yourself

Take yourself on a date. Don't wait for someone to come along to do something you want to. Treat yourself to a special date, flowers and all!

Do something by yourself around other people (dine in a restaurant, attend an exhibit). How do you feel? Do you feel left out, or is there a sense of adventure?

Do something childlike. You can go to a zoo, a matinee, an amusement park.

Volunteer your time if you are concerned about being alone.

Make sure you are spending quality time with yourself. You are worth it! List thirty things you can do by yourself that you enjoy doing. Remember this list whenever the panic hits you.

Chapter Summary

You are the only person who can please yourself 100 percent of the time.

You are the totality of your existence.

Celebrate you!

SECTION II

Introduction

By now you have determined your lifestyle, what you want out of life, and the qualities of the person you want to share it. Return to Meet a Mate, and tell the clerk, "I am looking for a man who is funny, sensitive, under 50, over 30, attractive, physically fit, and desirous a lifelong partner. "Bingo — your selection appears. Absurd ... maybe. However, the whole single world is a meet-a-mate, and your world (as large or small as you make it) is the Super Shopping Center. Once you decide your real goals, the selection process becomes an integral part of your life. Realizing that you are the only person who can take charge of your life gives you incredible power and freedom! If it is important to you, then you can now quit waiting for someone to place this person in your life. You now know it is up to you. This gives you the power to take the action steps that will correspond to your intended results.

Social situations designed solely to meet other single people might make you uncomfortable. If this happens, try to remember that everyone else also has feelings and insecurities. These are social activities you should take advantage of. Also, you need to introduce other pertinent activities into your agenda. When you are doing things you really enjoy, your single-stigma facade will fall away, and you will shine through.

One of the main keys is exposure. The saying goes, "If you throw enough spaghetti against the wall, some of it is bound to stick." (At least that's what my mother told me.) In sales, it is called the Law of Large Numbers, and it works. As I stated earlier, the more people you meet, the more you increase your chances of meeting someone you really like and making new friends. Remember that to know someone you have to meet them.

Often, this will mean taking the initiative. If you go to a function and sit by yourself without speaking to others, it won't help. If you are uncomfortable approaching and talking to strangers, you might try attaching yourself to whoever is doing the greeting or organizing. They will think nothing of introducing you to new people. Each strategy explores a limited number of actions you can take pertaining to it. There is room for you to jot down your notes also. These notes and ideas will be carried forward into the next chapter when we develop an action calendar. Keep an open mind, and have fun!

Chapter Eleven: Fun

It is important to enjoy yourself while you are looking for someone to complement your life. Meeting people should be exciting and enjoyable. If you are happy or excited, you look your best. Radiating a well-being will excite and attract people. People *want* to be with others who are happy with themselves and show it through their zest for life.

In the following exercise you will determine some of the activities you enjoy. Come back from time to time and expand on this list with new ideas that come to you.

List ten activities that you enjoy doing presently, have enjoyed in the past, or feel you would like to try. Review your personal profile if you need help brainstorming, or answer the following questions:

What are your favorite sports and hobbies?

What magazines, television and radio shows, and books do you enjoy?

List the last three things you did with great enjoyment.

If you had a month to do anything you wanted (no restrictions) what would you do?

(Place each idea you have on the ACTIVITY lines, and go on to the next)

ACTIVITY:
Rating:
Where do you find this:
Who participates:
Offshoot activities:

ACTIVITY:
Rating:
Where do you find this:
Who participates:
Offshoot activities:

ACTIVITY:
Rating:
Where do you find this:
Who participates:
Offshoot activities:

ACTIVITY:
Rating:
Where do you find this:
Who participates:
Offshoot activities

ACTIVITY:
Rating:
Where do you find this:
Who participates:
Offshoot activities:

ACTIVITY:
Rating:
Where do you find this:
Who participates:
Offshoot activities:

Make sure these activities are truly enjoyable for you. Go back through your list, and see yourself participating in each activity. How do you feel about it? On a scale of one to ten, does it rate nearer to the ten side? Make sure the action incites interest, enthusiasm, or a smile. Anything below a six toss out, you can replace it later. You want to meet others while *enjoying yourself in the process!*

Expand on what you have written with the first activity you listed. For example, perhaps you listed snow skiing. Where do you meet people who ski? Your first thought might be in order to meet people who like to ski, you need to spend considerable funds and travel to the slopes. Maybe it is the middle of July, and you feel you would have to wait six months for ski season. This is not necessarily true. Think of how this or any other activity could be associated. Is this the type of activity that people would form a club or association with meetings, discussions and other events? Isn't the off-season the time to buy equipment? Couldn't you go to the big off-season sales? Who participates in this sport? Probably physically active people. Where do you find them? What are some offshoot activities? Many people who ski also windsurf and water ski. Are these activities that you might enjoy or have interest in? Go back to your activity list. Fill in the question of where you might find this activity. In this example, the logical beginning would be the ski slopes.

Now, take the next two questions and brainstorm! Who are these people, and what else might they be doing?

This exercise serves to open your mind to the possibilities available. Possibilities are unlimited if you see them as so. Engaging in activities in which people interact gives everyone an easy way to talk and interrelate with each other. It would be difficult to join a dance club and never speak with your dance partners. If you are enjoying yourself, even when you don't meet someone, you are ahead. You are doing what you like and taking charge of what you want.

In the following section we will address methods of meeting new friends. Since everyone is an individual, different ideas and methods will appeal to different people. When you view this list, keep an open mind! Let your imagination associate freely to develop new ideas that will work for you! Don't wait until there is someone in your life. Participate, participate, participate and participate in your comfortable areas. By doing so, you are expressing your own worth, today!

Chapter Summary

People want to be with others who have a zest for life.

Don't wait until you find someone to enjoy your life.

You are worth enjoying it now.

Doing what you really like adds energy and creativity to your life.

Chapter Twelve: Strategies

This section of strategies focuses on you and your attitudes, attributes, and skills and how you can use them and embellish them. Some topics may seem elementary, but before you pass one by, be sure you are exhibiting it in your life. If you aren't, try to honestly examine yourself to see if you couldn't experience some improvement by adopting it into your life. Everyone has some room for improvement, so try approaching these with the attitude that you too could use a little adjusting.

Smile

What makes a person approachable? A simple smile works wonders. Think of a time someone genuinely smiled at you, for no apparent reason. It probably made you feel great, didn't it? A genuine open smile develops rapport and makes you more approachable and others more comfortable. You make them feel welcome. The added bonus is that it makes you feel great too. Try this: Practice your smile on everyone you meet. It could be the grocery checker, the gas-station attendant, the receptionist at your dentist office, or the great-looking woman standing in front of you. See if the way people react to you doesn't dramatically change. People love to feel special, and if you are smiling at them, they will and so will you.

ACTION STEPS

Each day for a week take time to notice and smile at someone you normally ignore or don't see.

Next time you are feeling particularly grouchy, smile at the next five people you see. Chances are your appearance and attitude will drastically change.

NOTES

Appearance

Do you present your best appearance to the world? When you take time to look your best, you naturally feel better about yourself. This translates into confidence. This doesn't necessarily mean picture perfect, but taking an extra few moments to check your appearance pays off in greater dividends. Would you want to meet yourself? If you did, would you be thinking about the wrinkled shirt, scraggly hair, or carelessly applied makeup on this person standing in front of you? Beauty to the point of perfection can be an obsession, but an attractive appearance, which translates into self-esteem, is always welcome. Be willing to show yourself and the world your best.

ACTION STEPS

Every day for one week, before you go out, check your appearance more carefully than usual. See yourself from the viewpoint of someone meeting you for the first time. What could use improvement?

Take time to add one special touch each morning, and see if you don't like the person you project even more.

NOTES

Self-Confidence And Reliance

How you feel about yourself is expressed in every aspect of your life, especially in your presentation of yourself. Do you project a confident, self-assured person? Or do you mumble, lose eye contact, slump, or generally look uncomfortable? People are attracted to individuals who exude self-confidence and self-assurance. This can be learned, just like any skill you possess. It simply takes practice.

Why not try something you have only dreamed about. Intimidation may have held you back from activities such as skydiving, scuba diving, or public speaking. However, doing it, whatever it is, will give you an expanded sense of confidence and self-belief. This may be the boost you need to start that conversation or extend that invitation to someone. You may find yourself saying, "If I had the gumption to do X (jump from an airplane, give a public speech, walk through a fire pit...), then certainly I can ask that person to lunch!"

ACTION STEPS

Write down any activities you have wanted to do but haven't done because some degree of fear held you back. Pick something from the list, and do it! The power and confidence that comes from this exercise is incredible.

Try talking to yourself in the mirror. Many well-known and respected public speakers practice this exercise before every speaking engagement. See yourself conducting a conversation that is important to you. What are you projecting, and how are you saying it? Keep doing this exercise until you are comfortable. If you are still unsure, ask a friend to help you. Being in a supportive environment gives you the security factor to be your most confident.

NOTES

Who You Are: Your Introduction Speech

Have you ever met someone, talked with them, answered their questions, and, as they walk away, kicked yourself for not saying something catchy or being more interesting? Have you had the reverse happen to you? You really want to meet the person across the room. They seem so alive and interesting. You get up the nerve and introduce yourself. As you talk with them, it seems they have very little to say or say it poorly, and you feel let down as you walk away. What could be happening is simply stage fright.

Through various exercises you have completed, you should now understand what an interesting person you really are. Introduce this fascinating person to others. Presentation is extremely important. Remember, you make only one first impression.

ACTION STEPS

If you could say or do anything, how could you present yourself in the most favorable light? Take into consideration your manner, speech, and actions. Write your fantasy introduction, the one that always comes to mind after you walk away from a conversation. It might be filled with enthusiasm, charisma, or witty remarks. You may want to explain some of the excitement or enjoyable aspects surrounding your job, your life, your hobbies, or your interests.

To compose this introduction, remember questions people have asked you in the past and how you responded. Then, remember how you wish you had! After writing these down, write the reply that you wish you had made.

Think back on people you have met in the past who impressed you. What was it that drew you to them, their smile, their composure, their sense of humor or their introduction and conversation? Create with words an introduction that conveys your and special qualities. Try practicing this in your mirror. As you become more comfortable, enlist a friend to listen and offer constructive hints and suggestions.

NOTES

Being A Great Conversationalist

Making others comfortable through the use of your conversational skills gives you the opportunity to see others at their best, when they are comfortable, talking and communicating. People love to be with individuals who make them feel witty and special. The first lesson to learn when working on your conversation skills is listening. People want to feel special, and you can do that by really listening to what they have to say, not just trying to get your own particular point across. An inconsiderate way to turn someone off is to feign interest while your mind and eyes wander. Everyone is aware when you are doing this. If someone bores you, excuse yourself, but there is no excuse for poor manners.

Another trait of a good conversationalist is the ability to develop rapport. This is simply finding common interests, usually by asking people questions to open them up. If inquiring about someone's occupation doesn't seem to create enthusiasm, try asking about hobbies or sports. This gives someone a chance to open up to you. Thus, you avoid the usual opening lines of name, rank, and job description.

ACTION STEPS

Next time you meet someone who appears shy, take the initiative to open them up. Ask questions, and then genuinely listen to their replies.

If you meet someone who interests you yet their conversation appears boring, give them a second chance. Do this by using your new conversation skills to find something they are excited talking about. Who knows, you may find a diamond in the rough!

NOTES

Imagination

The purpose of using your imagination in this context is to break away from limited thinking and typical behaviors. This will encourage you to experience life more fully, alone or with others. The added bonus is that people who use their imagination are noticed by the rest of the world. Standing out as untypical only gets you noticed and appreciated. By using your imagination to brainstorm, more and more creative thoughts come to you. You will probably find it interesting to ask other people about ways they have met people. Many of the stories you will come across will astonish and entertain you!

A good friend of mine is creative and adventurous. One evening she was walking into a local pub to meet a girlfriend. In front of the club was a beautiful convertible Jaguar. On an impulse, she decided to meet the person who owned that car. She wrote down the license number and description. Then, she went to the D.J. and told him the lights had been left on. She then posted herself at the door to watch who went out. It turned out to be an attractive woman in her early forties. When the woman came back in, my friend approached her and told her what she had done. She then offered to buy her a drink. They had a great laugh and became friends.

ACTION STEPS

This exercise is best done with a friend. If you are working on it alone, try to remember not to judge whatever to your mind, just write it down. Ask yourself or each other these questions and then follow the stream of thought that naturally follows.

The most boring date of your life...Why? The most exciting date of your life ... Why? What are five activities you have always wanted to do on a date. (Examples: browse through a museum, moonlight beach picnic ...) Now write down three related activities. (Browse through a museum ... go to an art auction, do a comparison tour of the galleys in an area, take an art-appreciation course ...)

Now, stretch even further and relate one more idea to each of your activities. (Example: "Browse through a museum" becomes "Attend a reception party at a local museum.")

Be open to new ideas, no matter how bizarre!

You might want to read "A Sign of the 80s" (Parent). It is the most hilarious story you may ever read of two women using their collective imagination to meet men.

NOTES

Keeping An Open Mind

An open mind is a sure way of maintaining an exciting and fun schedule. You don't have to say yes to every offer (some crazy) that comes your way. However, at least consider all aspects. Refusing an invitation because it is not something you normally do or know how to do will keep you in a rut. You never know what might broaden your horizons! Jeopardizing yourself isn't smart, so always use your common sense. Keep looking at the world with an open mind and open heart. This will surely help keep you young at heart. It will also increase your perspective on the world.

ACTION STEPS

Look through local event calendars until you find something that you think is totally outrageous, and GO! Keep an open mind. Probably you will learn something or at least have a great adventure!

Being too judgmental is negative to any relationship. Always let time and events precede a final negative judgment.

Relax. Everyone is his own person. Your ultimate partner will also have to adjust to you too.

NOTES

Visualization

First, create the world you want to live in. Then, live it. Generally, people react to outside influences rather than act on their own inner vision.

Visualizing is clearly seeing what you want in your life in order to help create it. By using your imagination with a completely focused outcome, you create for yourself complete clarity of thought. You can then hold this vision until it appears in your life. Using the vision as a conscious and empowering key to your life, you can quickly move past barriers that once seemed insurmountable. This technique teaches you to harness your natural imagination to help do your bidding for you. It is often said that the subconscious mind does not know the difference between fact and vivid imagination. Visualization tells your subconscious a story about what you see in your life. The more your unconscious mind believes in the visualization, the greater its ability to act upon it and draw it to you. This will happen through new ideas, seemingly random events, and the new awareness you set up in your inner mind. Just as you set your financial or physical goals and then see yourself acting them out, you can set and visualize your relationship goals by clearly seeing what you desire and then focusing your positive energy on it.

Suppose you have met someone you would like to invite to lunch. You reach for the phone, and fear raises its head. What if she says no? You put the receiver back down and think to yourself, "I will call later." Later, it only seems more difficult.

Take the same scenario. This time though, before you reach for the phone, you visualize the outcome. Taking a few relaxing breaths, you see yourself dialing the number and the other person answering the phone. "Hello, this is Rick," you say with a smile. "Remember me? We met at the art league Thursday evening." You see Joan smile and say, "Hi, of course I remember you. We discussed the upcoming auction." Your conversation is launched. Then take your image a step further and see the two of you lunching together, smiling and talking as you enjoy each other's company. With that outcome, what is to keep you from calling? Confidently hold your desired image in your mind as you dial the phone.

Mind games? Not really. The more you are able to visualize an outcome the more likely you are to create it. Read or listen to tapes by almost any great achiever and hear them say, "Set a goal, and see it completed." Doing this on a day-to-day basis gives you the capacity and know-how to create your desires on a larger scale.

Use this process to form your entire life as you want it. Go back to the goals you wrote earlier, and compose your own story around them. Our example is someone who would like to earn $120,000 yearly, wear a size 6 dress, live by the ocean and experience her perfect relationship. Already, with only that description, you are probably able to formulate a picture in your mind. The picture she forms is that of seeing herself awaken to a kiss from the wonderful man in her life. He brings her coffee in bed, and together they watch the sun rise over the ocean. In a short while they arise, and she goes to her closet to choose her clothes for the day. As her hand runs through her beautiful wardrobe, she sees the size 6 on the labels. She dresses and joins her husband for breakfast and some loving conversation. She then leaves for work, driving her new Mercedes. She sees herself in her large office, doing whatever it is she does for a living. Since it is payday, she sees herself picking up her check and depositing it into her bank. As she does, she glaces over her other accounts, CD's and a money market fund. She then drives home to share an intimate dinner with her lover.

Make your image as clear as possible, using as many of your senses as you can. Not everyone sees a clear picture, some people simply feel the essence surrounding the visualization. However you do it, bring as much life as possible to your image. You may want to smell the salt air, hear the voice of your lover talking softly to you, or feel yourself driving your car.

Go through your visualization when you are relaxed. Simply take a few deep breaths to unwind, and see your muscles resting easily and effortlessly.

When you finish your visualization, make a declaration such as, "This or something better now comes to me. Thank you!" Using the affirmations that you wrote earlier in conjunction with your visualization is even more powerful. Together the two techniques set up an energy field that resonates your success.

ACTION STEPS

Allow quiet time daily for your visualization to take place. Bring as many senses into play as you can. This is your daydreaming/life planning time, so use it to your best ability.

NOTES

Much of our world is now designed with ease of communication in mind. This is extremely helpful for the single person attempting to meet people. Think of what the world would be like if we lived without telephones and answering machines. Or what if we still lived mainly on farms and in rural areas, miles apart from friends and acquaintances. In this section we look at a few of the means of communication available to us today and how to apply these to our endeavors.

Networking

Into our lives come wonderful people some we keep, while others for some reason, disappear. Your friends, family, and acquaintances form a perfect networking machine.

It is easy to convey to someone what you want without appearing "desperate." Over lunch you can mention that you are taking a new tack in dating and explain to your lunch partner the qualities of the person you have decided to meet. By stating exactly what you want, you establish yourself as someone in control of your life.

A friend of mine, Sharon, took this suggestion to heart. She went through her address book and made contact with people she had not spoken with in six months or more. She chose only the people she remembered as having positive traits she could relate to. Each week she would place calls to some of these people until she made a lunch date. Sometimes this took one call, other times three or four. One Wednesday she met with a lady who had attended a class with her the year before. Sharon let this woman know that not only was her purpose for calling to cultivate old friendships but to cultivate new ones also. She went on to explain how she was taking charge of meeting someone and described the traits she was looking for in a man. Her friend listened and then replied, "My brother has recently moved into town. He is similar to the person you are describing to me. He is a wonderful man, and I would enjoy the three of us having dinner together." A week later they met for dinner. The chemistry was apparent from the first hello.

ACTION STEPS

If you feel that these types of people are limited in your life, use the following checklist to trigger your own contact list.

Begin with your address books, past and present
Look through your rolodex. List the family members you enjoy being with. What clubs and organizations have you attended? Who did you meet? What friends have you lost contact with? What about friends of friends? Do you have job contacts you have lost touch with? What about friends you may have had in college or high school?

List every person who comes to mind. Later you can go through and determine who you really want to contact. You can also invite these people to attend functions and activities you don't want to attend alone. Don't expect instant results. People usually need gentle reminding to keep you in mind. Meet people and join people in their functions with an open mind. You never know where or how you will meet someone you want to know!

Decide on a schedule of contacting these people, and stick to it.

NOTES

Buddy System

Support systems are an integral part of most peoples lives. We begin with the family unit and continue into our friendships. Some of us get married and become a part of a new family team. If divorce comes along, this new support team is shattered, hopefully we have friends and family to fall back on. We use our friendships to help each other by listening to problems, worries, and ideas and making suggestions. Among your friends is at least one person with whom you can form a buddy system. A buddy system is a small team designed exclusively to support one another in achieving each other's desires. A buddy can offer suggestions, cheer you on, prod you when you need it, and help to celebrate your successes. A buddy can help make you feel wanted when things start getting you down.

Here are a few ground rules for choosing your buddies. Don't pick someone who wants the *exact* same thing you do. This could create competition. A man and woman who are strictly good friends and looking for someone in their lives make an excellent team. Be sure you are only friends. If the other person has designs on you, this won't work! A man and woman together are disarming, and they can approach anyone easily. The drawback here is the possibility of being perceived as a couple. So be sure that you know how to present yourselves. Another possibility is a friend of the same sex with a different agenda. An example is a married friend trying to lose weight, recovering from an addiction, or finding the perfect job. With a buddy, it may be easier to go into unfamiliar places and to talk with people you may not know. Find a buddy, and help each other achieve!

ACTION STEPS

List everyone you know who would make a potential buddy. Keep your eyes open for others. A blind date could turn into a great supporting friend if the passion isn't there.

A program is available through most Unity churches called "Master Mind." It is a support group that follows the outline and journal written by Jack Bowland. Start up a team, and begin supporting each other!

NOTES

Business Card Or Calling Card

In the business world you would not consider approaching prospects without a business card. You need to convey who you are and how they can reach you. Business cards are the accepted solution. If you normally carry a business card, use it. It is the easiest nonthreatening way to give or receive a phone number. "Here is my card. Give me a call and we can have lunch sometime" or "Do you have a card?" If you are not comfortable receiving calls at your office, offer to jot down your home number.

What if you don't carry a business card or have a job? Make one up! Do you have a hobby you could connect yourself to? Possibly you are (or would like to be) a free lance artist or a cooking consultant. What about a tasteful card with just your name and number? Isn't that better than something scribbled on a napkin? It is definitely more dignified and not as easily lost or run through the washing machine. If you need to have a card made be sure to take time to really think it through and project the image you want.

Any knowledgeable printer can show you paper types and type styles to correspond with the image you want. You may want to have personal note cards printed at the same time. If you send someone a note, don't send your card. It will look too much like business correspondence.

Having your own personalized calling card will also serve as a great conversation piece. Regardless of whether or not you feel it is pushy, people will remember you.

ACTION STEPS

Always carry extra cards wherever you go.

Decide what will go on your card and what image you want to portray. You will find it much more helpful to go to a printer with your homework done.

NOTES

Answering Machine

Possibly one of the greatest mysteries of our time is how we existed B.A.M. (before answering machines). To be in the dating world, you definitely need one. People need to feel comfortable in reaching you. They get discouraged if they call three or four times and never get an answer or are unable to leave a message. Most people will be courteous enough to leave a message if you provide the means. Remember, when you are calling someone if you don't leave a message they will never know you called. Sounds pretty elementary, yet I am constantly amazed at the number of people who say to me, "I always call you but I never hear from you." I find that is because they have never left a message. How am I to know to call? When leaving a message, be sure to leave your number, even if you are positive they have it. The person you are calling may have misplaced it or not have it with them and might want to extend an invitation for that evening.

Answering machines vary from basic to high-tech. You need two features, the ability to receive clear messages and to retrieve your messages from a remote location, which will prove invaluable.

A good friend of mine shortly, after purchasing her first machine, reported a new malady. She referred to it as the Answering Machine Blues. This is what results when you are able to retrieve your messages only at home. Knowing that surely Prince Charming or at least Robert Redford has called, you excuse yourself early from dinner with friends and rush home. Upon arriving, you find that the little red light isn't blinking. Your heart sinks; no one called. After a few minutes you suddenly realize that the cat has obviously knocked the phone off the hook so no one could reach you. Yet when you check, you see the phone is on the hook. It is now too late to return to your friends, and, so you assume the phone-watching vigil. Get a machine, and let it do it for you!

ACTION STEPS

Shop around. Check all options and pricing before purchasing. You might want to look in the classified ads or at a garage sale for a quality used machine at a reduced price.

NOTES

After you have created in your mind what you want out of you life, and analyzed yourself, set up your support systems, all that is left is moving into action. Nothing will happen without you expending energy. The following are suggestions on where to go and what to do.

Groups

A friend of mine once jokingly told me that the results of a study he had conducted reveled that there are more interest and support groups in the world than there are individuals to attend. It's an exaggeration, maybe, but also a good illustration that if you want to find something to do or someone to do it with, just look around. There are numerous places that people congregate. Join them, visit them, volunteer your time, or experiment with them. Whatever suits your needs, somewhere there are people joining together for that same purpose. The following is a twenty-point checklist you can use to strike a memory or create new ideas. Some of these have been elaborated on in the following section. Some are left up to you.

Alumni groups
Art leagues, societies, and supporters
Business associations and networks
Civic groups
Clubs and associations for almost any purpose (dancing, skiing...)
Cultural groups
Environmental groups
Fund-raising groups and events
Health-related groups
Hobbies
Political associations
Religious groups
Singles groups
Self-expansion groups
Sports (play or sponsor)
Support for almost anything (AA, Al-Anon, Single parents...)
Union groups
Vocational groups
Volunteer groups
Youth groups (Big Brother/Big Sister...)

ACTION STEPS

To find one of these organizations, try any of the following: chamber of commerce, religious affiliations, libraries, community centers, bulletin boards, yellow pages, schools, newspapers, newsletters, magazines, single organizations, friends, acquaintances, and your office.

NOTES

Private Clubs

Each private club targets a specific membership type. Sometimes this is written in black and white. Usually, though, you need to do a little research to find out. An example in our area is two private yacht clubs. Although they appear similar from the outside, if you ask members and employees, you would find that there are distinct differences. One is a younger and more business-related club while the other is traditional and caters to those who are more socially oriented. Most private clubs center on sports such as golf, tennis, and yachting.

One advantage of a private club is the immediate acceptance factor. Once you become a member you are usually accepted into the fold and become part of the family. People often find it is easy to talk with other members because they have common interests and already have an introduction via the club.

When meeting with the membership salesperson, be candid (without being blatant) as to what you are looking for. Inquire about the membership make-up, and size, an average member profile, and what age group the club caters to. Check to determine if it mostly a married crowd or if single people carry memberships. Is there a large socially active group, or do just a few people regularly participate in activities. Is the crowd cliquish or open? Remember, the person you are talking with has a job to recruit new members and could be anticipating what you would like to hear, instead of what you need to know. Ask if you can attend a member function before you join. Most clubs will allow it.

Finally, ask yourself if this is something you would really enjoy doing. Are you financially capable of covering the costs without over-extending your budget? Is it something you would enjoy for several years? Initiation fees vary, but many are a substantial investment. Also, take into consideration the ability to sell your membership if you desire.

Note to women: Many single men belong to sports-related private clubs. If there is a sport you enjoy, such as golf, tennis, or sailing, you would probably want to investigate a membership. Frequently, clubs have junior or individual memberships with limited privileges (non-voting) that are substantially less expensive than other memberships.

ACTION STEPS

Could a private club be for you? Is it something that you could ask your business/employer to share costs with? Check into clubs in your area for information and pricing. Is there anything that appeals to you?

NOTES

Health Clubs

In many ways, health clubs are beginning to replace the bar scene as people become more health-conscious and join clubs where they can improve their bodies and life expectancy. In order to keep abreast of these changes, many fitness clubs have changed formats and most clubs are now coed. As you shop around, you will find that each club has a different personality. Talk with the people working there and those working out. Is it a comfortable place where people talk among themselves? Or, is it a serious bodybuilding and weight-training club? What are you looking for? The personal benefits you will receive from joining a club should be your main consideration. A note of caution: Don't join a gym because someone you are dating or want to date works out there. Too many times friends of mine have paid initiation fees and joined, only to find themselves uncomfortable when they are no longer dating the person who is working out there. Join for your personal gain. Any fringe benefits are just that!

ACTION STEPS

Take an assessment of your fitness level and appearance.

Determine what you would like to change. Talk with trainers at your local gyms and health clubs to decide which would be most beneficial to you, and develop a schedule you can live with and build upon. Congratulate yourself for your efforts, don't get discouraged and give up, it usually takes a month or so to see any results!

NOTES

Vacationing Alone (Or With A Friend)

Consider traveling somewhere on your own. Just you, a few clothes, your ticket, or your car. If you try this, you should have an enjoyable adventure. Your agenda is entirely your own. No one to check plans with or disagree on sight-seeing with.

You might wonder how this would help you to meet someone. There is always a slight chance you might meet someone while traveling. More so, traveling alone can build your confidence. It will help you to recognize you are developing your life on your own.

You should discover that while you are looking for a partner, you can still be a whole person, leading a full and exciting life.

Another vacation avenue is through one of the many groups now catering to single people. They can be found through your travel agent or by calling a local singles group. Many single-related publications also advertise these travel groups. Club Med has offered singles-only vacations for quite some time. Before you make your reservations or pay a deposit, check on the agent to ascertain that they can deliver on their promises. If you aren't comfortable traveling alone, consider a trip with a platonic friend or possibly schedule one with your buddy. You might find this to be more fun then you imagined.

ACTION STEPS

Make a list of places you have always wanted to go.

Is there anywhere on the list you would be comfortable going by yourself?

Commit to taking a short trip.

Talk with a travel agent or a single travel group.

Ask for references from people who have already taken the group trip, and get their input.

NOTES

Parties And Receptions

When you throw a party, always ask your guests to bring a friend. You may ask them to invite only single people, or it may not really matter. Have a party to meet your neighbors. I met a lady who had just gotten married. When asked how long she and her husband had known each other, she said about two years. However, she added, they saw each other every day for about four years before that. Actually, they lived directly across the street from each other but had never spoken! Finally, they met through a block party. Many of us live in an unsociable and untouchable world and rarely know the people next door. Organizing a block party is not only a great way to meet your neighbors but also a good method of crime prevention. Many communities are now encouraging people to meet their neighbors this way. Call your local police department. Several departments are helping to organize and sponsor such parties. If you know your neighbors, it becomes easier to detect any unusual or suspicious activity around a home.

Another great place to make friends is your office. One of the best office-party ideas came from an another friend of mine. Newly divorced, he was working in a branch office of a large company. He begin inviting people to meet after work and calling the meetings office seminars. They quickly became popular. They would meet twice a month, always on an off night and in a quiet pub or out-of-the-way bar. Everyone was asked to bring a friend from *outside* the company. Not only were company friendships formed and communications improved, but also, outside friendships developed. The party notification was done via interoffice mail using crazy themes on fliers.

ACTION STEPS

In order to organize office parties, point out to the employer how the level of camaraderie and team building will increase. Who knows, the employer may sponsor them.

It is fairly easy to be invited to receptions. Suppose you enjoy art and would like to meet someone who is also artistically oriented. Call your local museum and ask for a membership package. Usually the price of membership is nominal, and functions are held throughout the year. While you are meeting people, you will also be enjoying yourself, enhancing your life, and developing your interests. Check your local library or chamber of commerce to find a particular interest group. The library will have a reference book entitled The Encyclopedia of Associations. You will discover groups you never dreamed existed. This should open your horizons to new possibilities.

NOTES

Finding The "In" Places And The "In" People

You will find it beneficial to acquaint yourself with someone who is active in the single scene. This could be someone who belongs to several singles groups, organizes parties, or is a volunteer matchmaker. This is a person who takes pride in knowing what is going on and where.

This person also knows some things you will never find in the local papers, such as the accidental in-the-know spot and when to be there. In our city, there is a time that singles go to a certain grocery store, a particular hardware store, and a certain park in which they jog or walk their dog. Some more aggressive individuals borrow dogs. People with dogs always talk to one another.

You will find this person by asking. If you are with a singles group, find out who is organizes most of the activities. Someone is bound to put you in contact with the person who seems to know everything that is going on. Simply learning the right places and times and being on the will-call list of this person can be helpful and fun.

ACTION STEPS

Acquaint yourself with whoever you need to know. You'll make a good friend in the process!

NOTES

Churches, Synagogues, And Other Centers Of Worship

People who enjoy similar spiritual and religious beliefs often have other common interests too. Many of these groups and affiliations have single and social functions with outside activities. If you are already attending such a group and feel that you know everyone in your particular place of worship, try a different one. It could be the same denomination but across town, or you may be interested in what other groups have to offer and this is a perfect time to look. As lifestyles go through a subtle shift back to the family unit, places of worship are becoming more popular. This is a natural progression of conscience. Consequently, there are more and more single people attending these services. Not only can you meet people with common interests and beliefs, you will probably find a wonderful support network.

ACTION STEPS

If you don't presently attend a church or spiritual gathering, consider changing that pattern. Frequently, as children and teenagers, we are turned off by the spiritual group of our parents. Investigate various groups. You do not have to attend the church your parents chose for you.

If your particular group doesn't have a singles organization and you think it needs one, start it. You can probably receive help with this from similar organizations that have already done the groundwork.

NOTES

Teaching

What special skills do you have that others would like to acquire? Try your hand at teaching. A friend of mine owns a restaurant. She holds monthly cooking lessons (at her restaurant, of course) for a hefty fee. You get to eat what you cook! This is great exposure for the restaurant.

Another friend of mine teaches a foreign-language course, the same one she is also studying! Her objective is to learn by doing. The fringe benefit is that she never lacks for dates. She is in great demand among those she teaches (mostly businessmen in rising positions in their companies). In most cities there are many different study courses, and you can teach almost anything in the world. If you don't believe this, pick up a schedule from some of these groups. You will be amazed at the variety of courses available.

By teaching at a community college, another friend of mine has developed a large business around teaching and renting windsurfers. It goes on and on. If you have a skill, there is someone in the world who would like to learn it, and you will meet new people in the process.

ACTION STEPS

Look through local schools, universities, and the yellow pages under adult education classes. See what is being taught and if there are any groups you can teach for or any ideas you get.

Make a list of your skills, and call one of these colleges to inquire into the need for your particular skills.

NOTES

"What's Happening" File

Periodically (weekly is best) scan any and all papers, magazines, newsletters, bulletin boards, other area you can find with information about upcoming events and happenings in your areas of interest. Eithcr write this chosen information down on a calendar you view often or start a file. Be certain that you organize the events sequentially and view it often. This file will serve to inform you of potential dates on local happenings.

ACTION STEPS

Subscribe to any service you believe will be helpful. The ease of information coming directly into your hands is well worth the few dollars the subscriptions will cost you.

NOTES

Maintaining records of our goals and successes allows us to relate to our progress. It also allows us to see all that we are accomplishing and to congratulate ourselves.

We must also keep in mind that meeting other people and taking the initiative to do this can put some stress into our lives. If we realize this and make allowances for it, then that little fearful voice inside can relax a little!

Another point to remember is that if we don't follow through with what we are doing, then very little will be truly accomplished. So, see where you are, give yourself a break, and then follow through on what you have begun!

Following Through

If you follow through in anything you set out to accomplish, your chances of success are much greater. Following through on your actions is simply taking the next step and then the one after that. Say you meet someone at a party, and since you enjoy the conversation, you exchange cards before parting. Next, unfortunately what happens often is that you leave the conversation, feeling buoyant. You have introduced yourself to someone, you engaged in conversation and you exchanged numbers. You tell yourself that you will call him for lunch soon as you walk away. The next day dawns. Well, you think to yourself, it is probably too soon to call. I will do it tomorrow. Tomorrow comes and goes in a flurry of business. So does the next day. It is now the fourth day. The memory is a little fuzzy. Did he really want me to call, or was he just being nice? Did I really find him attractive, or was it just that there was no one else to talk with? What if we don't have anything to say to each other? What if he doesn't remember me? If you are a female you may feel it is too pushy to call. Maybe it seems too soon to call — you don't want to look desperate. What if he is a bore? What if I am?

The longer you go without calling, the more likely you are to drown in negative what if's. Eventually so much time has passed you will be embarrassed to call or they may really not remember you (especially if it is two years later!). Lack of follow through can usually be traced to two things: apathy or fear of rejection. If it is apathy, you need to relook at what you really want. For most people, though, it is fear of rejection, pure and simple. What if they say no? Or worse, what if they don't even remember me?

One way to counteract this is to make yourself memorable when you do call. Bring up some point that will remind them of you and the conversation. It could be how or where you met or something about you they connected with ("Hi, this is Sally. We met at Suzan's party"..."Hi, this is Sally. We met when you were admiring my car"...) If you follow up with everyone you meet, you may eventually experience some form of rejection. What appears to you to be rejection probably isn't that at all to the other person. They could be too shy or too scared to build a friendship, or maybe they are already in a relationship and somehow didn't convey that to you. You never know where someone else stands until you ask them or they tell you, and you never get an answer until you pose a question.

ACTION STEPS

When you do call someone, remember a few ground rules. First, check to make sure she can talk, that she isn't busy at that moment. If she is, she may appear rushed and could give you the impression that she doesn't want to talk to you when really you just caught her at a inconvenient time. Next, give her a choice of two specific activities (lunch or racquetball). Choose something nonthreatening (lunch verses dinner on a saturday night) and with a specific time duration (lunch, seminar, or a sporting event). The less it looks like a first date the less threatening it is. Give people time to get to know you before dates begin looking like dates. If you feel you are too shy to just call someone, you may want to send a card or a note. This may seem to be a strange way to reintroduce yourself, but if you don't do anything, a potential friend may fall through the cracks.

NOTES

Motivation, Maintenance, And Rewards

Keeping yourself motivated and on schedule is an important aspect of accomplishing your goals. How do you stay motivated? Is it strictly the outcome and completion of your goal, or does rewarding yourself along the way help? At one time, I wanted to lose fifteen pounds. I would lose a little and sometimes gain a little back. Fifteen pounds seemed so far away, and I really wasn't motivated.

One day while browsing through the mall I found a pair of pants I really wanted. They were stylish and would be a great addition to my wardrobe. I could see they would be flattering to someone who weighed eight to ten pounds less than I did! I purchased them anyway. Then I hung them next to my mirror along with two matching jackets. They provided the incentive I needed. Although the long-term goal had been important to me, it hadn't been tangible enough to provide me with the push I needed. The pants were. I quickly dropped the weight and fit into the pants. With the momentum established, it was easy to reach my final goal.

ACTION STEPS

Decide on a reward system for yourself.

Write your rewards on your action calendar, and provide yourself with them as you complete your task. This will keep you focused on your goal and give you added incentive along the way.

NOTES

No "Shoulds" Allowed

If you are a shy person, taking the initiative to meet people may be a little overwhelming. Remember, when forcing yourself into action, don't forget to honor your needs and feelings. If you are taking steps to do something that is basically against your nature, you are not being true to yourself. Allow your comfort level and confidence to build up. The rule is, Stretch, don't break. Slowly build up to what you feel you should be doing. As you do this, you will realize that the only things you *should be doing are those that work for you.* You will see that if you force yourself, you will probably not be your natural self.

The more you are yourself and choose actions that are your own ideas, not someone else's idea of you, the more people you will meet who will enjoy you for who you are!

ACTION STEPS

Remember: stretch, don't break. If you push yourself past your maximum stretch point, you may find yourself pulling back completely. Monitor your actions and reactions to what you are doing, and listen to your inner voice.

NOTES

Keeping A Journal

Keeping a personal journal is a great method of charting your progress and recognize changes and evolutions. Although a journal can appear to be intimidating and time-consuming, it can really be fun and kept up easily and quickly. It is helpful to determine a minimum amount of time you care to spend working on this journal on a daily, weekly, or monthly basis — probably not less than once a week to develop a true perspective. I suggest a simple spiral notebook. You might want to start off by writing the date and briefly describing what is going on in your life and what you want to accomplish. You might include writing about any people in your life, how you feel about them, and about you, what you have been doing and any upcoming events.

The simple act of committing to writing is usually enough to get the words flowing. If you find yourself stuck, write down anything: lists, letters, stories, someone else's stories. Writing is self-perpetuating. A journal can serve as a wonderful pick-me-up when you need one. As you glance over what you have written, you will be pleased with the progress. I have kept a journal for the past ten years. It amazes me to look back through what I have written ten, five, even one year ago and how things have changed. Especially how I have accomplished what I set out to do. This also gives you the chance to engage in some self-dialogue. You can have discussions with yourself, work out questions that come to mind, or just chat and write lists for a while.

ACTION STEPS

Buy a notebook and commit to write the ebb and flow of your goals and actions.

NOTES

Single Services
Single services provide a important function. It doesn't really matter how you meet someone; the end result is what you are after. Use your best judgment, and never do something that you are uncomfortable with, no matter how well it may have worked for someone else. There are an estimated 23 million single people in the United States. As you look into these services, you will see innovative ways many single people are meeting each other. No matter what method you employ to meet people, remember to use your common sense. Meet in public places, never give your home address to a stranger, and, if possible, do not give your home number. You place the call. These are simple precautions. They will serve you well no matter what you are doing. Use your experience and common sense. If something doesn't feel right, don't do it! As the special needs of single people are recognized, more and more inventive means of meeting one another arise. The following is a list of a few of the services that are available. Under each are suggestions on how to find similar services in your local area.

Dating Services
These come in a variety of types. They are popular because you can meet so many people quickly. The trick is to maintain a positive attitude and keep meeting people. The only difference between dating services and you looking on your own is the dating service has done your homework for you. You have to take the action. There are video dating companies, computer dating services, phone lines to call, and companies that carry pictures and resumes. Look in your yellow-page directory under dating services or singles. Ask for referrals, and take your time in making a decision. Although most businesses are reputable, there may also be those more interested in your money. Use your best judgment. Also, look in your newspaper classified sections and single publications for ads.

Matchmakers
Matchmakers receive mixed reviews. The only way you can make this work for you is to be specific about what you want in a mate. No generalities. Share your want/wish list. Try the yellow-page directory under matchmaker. Unfortunately for these individuals, this is a hard service to advertise. You might try your local Jewish

community center. Although it may appear to be a stereotype, most of the best matchmakers I have met are Jewish and will work with all people. You might try checking with singles groups you come in contact with. Word-of-mouth is usually the best way to find a matchmaker. Services and pricing vary tremendously, so be sure to ask all of your questions before committing.

Single Publications, Personal Ads, And Telephone Ads
Check the newsstands. There are many local and national publications targeting only single people. Also, many local papers will have a personal ad section in the classifieds. The personal ads give you the opportunity to make contact by mail first. These publications also serve as a clearing-house for events and information. Single classified ads are becoming more and more accepted. Several people I know how had good results using and answering the ads. The newest twist are ads using the 1-900-numbers. These are actually legitimate ads placed by individuals. You can dial their particular extension and listen to a taped message about the person. In her book, Making Love Happen, Rebecca Sydnor gives many tips on writing and answering ads.

Single Clubs And Support Groups
Try your local yellow-page directory under single. Most of these groups are smaller though and will not be carrying an ad. Check with your chamber of commerce, which always has a wealth of information. Also, many religious affiliations have single organizations. Look in local newspapers, single publications, and bulletin boards for club meeting announcements. You will find that there is a large contingency of single people willing to help each other. They will help to point you in the direction of the group you are looking for. All you need to do is take the first step.

Chapter Thirteen: Action Calendar

*Power comes from completion,
and action is completion in motion.*

No matter how knowledgeable you are, how prepared you are, how ready for change you are, until you commit and move into action, nothing will happen. By deciding on the required actions and then staying with them, you are displaying your level of commitment. This is what the universe and individuals are looking for. Disappointments and delays are only small detours. They are opportunities to look at what is going on and what needs to be done. By looking at what works, doesn't work and where you can change, you can continually check your course for success.

Another problem people face when they finally decide to take action is overcommitting. They try to eat too many pieces of pie at once. This often happens around the beginning of the New Year, birthdays, or other significant dates, when an individual may feel his life needs improving. He decides to lose ten pounds, double his income, find the relationship, remodel his house, and learn yoga. All in the next three months.

All of these items are achievable. The problem comes in the scheduling. The first week of this all-consuming schedule requires a time commitment from 4:00 a.m. until 9:00 p.m. When can they find time to meet new people and develop relationships or simply stop and enjoy life? What happens the day the schedule isn't met? They may become self-deprecating and try driving harder or say, "What the hell I can't do all of that anyway." A hopeless feeling sets in, and they become overwhelmed. Realizing later that a week, a month, a year has gone by, and none of the dreams have been accomplished.

This is a easy trap to avoid. Simply take a lot of small steps that will add up to the completion of your goal. Almost anything can be accomplished if you have the needed information, know the steps required to get there, and then act on them.

In the preceding chapters, we acquired the information needed. Now it is time to determine the steps required. Here we will take into consideration only your relationship goals. Later, you can come back to this section and do this exercise with every area of your life in which you have goals to achieve.

The first determination is the priority of the goals. Is it the number one priority or something that could take three to five years to achieve? The degree of importance of a particular goal will determine the time and energy you are willing to spend to achieve it. Determine if it is it worth fifteen minutes, an hour, or two hours of your time daily. If you find it hard to set a specific time allowance, try committing to a certain number of steps each day.

The next consideration is a financial one because some activities and actions will require a monetary investment. Determine the amount you are willing to spend, and set a financial budget.

Now, go back through your marketing strategies. You should have somewhere between five and twenty tactics you have targeted for yourself and made notes on. On page 111 you will find a column titled Action. Write your strategies in this space. Then, number them in order of your preference and in order of the ability of the action to get you closer to your goal. An example is:

Kathy recently ended a long-term relationship. Although she feels better for being out of it, she is somewhat afraid and unsure on how to meet new people. She is overweight and self-conscious about it. She is not shy, but she knows that her conversational skills are limited. She has a close-knit group of friends (mostly women) and seldom moves outside of the group. As an accountant for an industrial firm, she does not carry a business card, and she is uncomfortable with creating her own. She would never write her number down and give to someone. However she might impulsively hand someone her card. She acknowledges that her weight problem is holding her back, and she feels unattractive. Having tried dieting and not gotten anywhere, she knows she needs to take more substantial measures. Improving her appearance will improve her confidence and attitude. Her top three preferences toward action steps are: using the buddy system, having a party, and improving her appearance. The three steps she feels will help the most are: improving her appearance, improve her ability to carry on a lively conversation, and joining a health club.

This clearly shows a need to improve her appearance and thus her self-confidence first. She can use the buddy system to achieve this by finding someone to support her. If she wants to have a party, she might do a trial run where she invites the friends she knows while she works on her appearance.

You see that even though you may be more comfortable doing a particular item, if you are honest with yourself, you know some other action may produce greater results thus reaping you greater rewards. Since there are some steps you are more comfortable with and some steps that reap greater benefits, you need to take a mix of the two.

Action Step	Order of Preference	Reward Status
1		
2		
3		
4		
5		
6		
7		
8		

Action Step	Order of Preference	Reward Status
9		
10		
11		
12		
13		
14		
15		

Now list every small step you will need in order to complete the larger action step. We will use Mike as an example. He has decided to join an organization around a sport he enjoys will be his first step. This will provide him with the benefit of doing something he enjoys while also associating with people who share enjoyment of the same sport. His action steps look like this:

Activity: Join a sports related group

(1) List every sport of interest
(6) find the one you like and join
(3) call and obtain information
(4) attend a trial meeting
(5) possibly attend a second meeting before committing
(2) determine what day and time you have available

He numbers them according to a logical progression. In this example, scheduling is a prime consideration. He is already busy in his job and usually entertains clients during lunch. He is also involved in volunteer work on Tuesday and Thursday evenings. He usually spends Monday evenings at home reading and working. Deciding that he is willing to attend a Wednesday, Friday, or weekend meeting, he is now free to begin gathering information. He will gather information on anything in which he has a genuine interest. If it doesn't fit his schedule, he can file it for future reference. In this example, he has given himself a month to complete this step. Since step one always comes before step two, and action one always comes before action two, the calendar is filled in like this.

ACTION STEPS

Attend at least four meetings to look for a group.

Invite one person to a social lunch each week. This can be someone I am interested in or someone who may be a contact.

Be sure to break each action down into steps, and then plot them on your daily calendar. Integrate this calendar into your present schedule. Complete your tasks each day. Every time you do, you will feel more in charge of your life, and you will see a direction beginning to take place. Power comes from completion. Just do it and don't stop to procrastinate.

Chapter Summary

Always see your ultimate goal.

Break it down until you see that it is manageable.

Set times and dates.

Do easier tasks first in order to build confidence.

When you have completed something, check it off your list. Psychologically, this will reward you for your accomplishments.

Ignore and disarm the critic in you. This friend/foe will do everything possible to point out why it is impossible for you to do what you set out to accomplish. We all have this nagging voice to one degree or another. When you hear it beginning to nag, write down what it is telling you. Write down your reply by telling it how and why you are going to do what you have set out to accomplish. Eventually this nagger will get tired of making no sense and shut up!

Visualize your outcome. Always see yourself where you plan on being. See it as if you are already there. You will achieve results faster using this technique.

All you need to reach your desired goal is knowledge of where you are going and the required steps to get there. Break these steps down into manageable units, take action.

Power comes from completion, so do it!

Chapter Fourteen: Rejection

Rejection generally strikes fear into our hearts. However, isn't it really just someone else making a decision that is different from the one we wanted them to make? How do you know what their decision is based on? Frequently, we take rejection personally. She must think I'm a bore, because she doesn't want to go out with me again. Maybe he doesn't like me, because he didn't dance with me when I asked him to. Now I am sure everyone saw me get turned down, and they are laughing at me behind my back. I am so embarrassed. Perhaps you don't know the whole story. Maybe he was lame or afraid of looking foolish on the dance floor but would have loved just talking with you.

Rejection is completely our own perception. It is based solely on how we see another's actions. What about the person who is not particularly attractive, yet never seems to lack for dance partners or dates? Could this person be one who doesn't let a "no" stop him from trying again and find someone else to focus on? Remember, everyone is on a different schedule, and it may not be the one you are on. Work on building your self-esteem. If you invite someone to lunch and they refuse, don't wallow in self-pity. Turn around and ask someone else, someone you know will say, "Yes, I would love to have lunch with you". You will keep yourself reinforced instead of beat up.

A girlfriend of mine told me a story recently of how she had been left by the man she had been dating. He had been seeing another woman on the sly, and had lead her on and then dumped her. She described how awful he was and on and on. Toward the end of the conversation, she said in an insincere tone, "I should thank her for taking him away. Now I can get on with my life." I knew that this relationship had been a cause of grief in her life for quite some time. She had refused to let go because she was afraid no one else was out there for her to meet.

She went on for some time about what a rat this man was and how awful she felt for having been rejected. Finally, I asked her if anything else was going on in her life. Oh, yes, and she launched into a conversation about all she had been doing, with both her female friends and her new male friends (three to be exact), the weight she had lost, and just the general good that was going on in her life. Yet in her mind things really weren't right because this man had left her.

She could have chosen instead to see real truth in what she had said. The new girlfriend really had done her a favor. My friend had gotten out of a relationship that had been a source of hurt for her for a long time. It had been a drag on her energy instead of an uplifting experience, yet she kept dragging this baggage around with her. There must be something wrong with me to let myself get into a relationship like that, to be dumped for another woman, or not to get asked out again, the list goes on and on.

The truth is how we see rejection is how it is. If you see it as proof of your lack of worth, then it is. You will be sure to carry that idea around with you, and others will pick up on it. If you see it as a learning experience, that's what it will be. What did you learn? Not to date left-handed people? Or rats? Or did you learn that next time you should get to know someone before you hand them your heart. Maybe you should listen to what you are being told. Someone may be telling you they aren't ready for a relationship but you don't hear them because it is not what you want.

Our society tends to look at the negative side of the world. Instead of birth announcements we have obituaries. Instead of an 80 percent chance of sunshine, it is a 20 percent chance of rain! We hear of all the people who are at war. Do you know that only about 1 percent of the world's population is actually at war? The emphasis on the negative is over the positive, and we carry that into our lives. Our perception is our reality. If someone you're interested in isn't returning the attraction, let him go. Accept him for what he is and where he is. Wish him the best. Then get on with your life. Know that what you really want is out there for you. If you have to kiss a few frogs along the way, then look at it as practice!

ACTION STEPS

Think back on past experiences you thought were bad. Write them down, and look for all the good that came out of them (examples: losing a job, a divorce, a theft).

When was the last time someone rejected you? Can you even remember? Is your life really affected today by that rejection? If you have someone you would like to approach but are afraid of being rejected, project yourself into the future. Would this rejection matter a month from now. Would you even remember it? Do you think the other person would. Does it matter?

NOTES

Chapter Summary

Rejection is all your perception!

Chapter Fifteen: Opportunity

Remember, without action, without expending energy, nothing can happen. You create your own opportunities by recognizing and acting upon them as they come to you. How do you know if you are being presented with a worthwhile opportunity? See how it feels inside. What is your gut instinct? You are now prepared to create your own opportunities. You have all the tools needed to do this.

Important point: once you create an opportunity, you must act upon it! This can't be emphasized enough.

You find yourself at the point where you feel you are ready for a wonderful relationship. By planning and work you have positioned yourself to meet people. You are at a function and meet someone you are extremely attracted to. You talk, laugh and then go your own way. That voice inside you is telling you to invite him to lunch, get a number, give a number - DO SOMETHING! But, you don't. Later, back at home you chastise yourself.

Why not take the initiative? I realize that this can be a scary feeling. You are making yourself vulnerable by putting yourself in a potential position for rejection, but so what? We know that rejection is only a perception. Underneath our individual exteriors, we are all very similar. Each person has fears, joys, and dreams. You may never know if someone you would like to meet feels the same way about you unless you ask. They may be afraid of your rejecting them!

While writing this book, I stopped and thought back over the people I had met and dated in my life. Almost everyone of them involved my taking a chance and inviting or responding to someone. It meant being open, being willing to talk with strangers.

Think for a moment over your past. Have there been times when you wanted to say something or do something but didn't, something you may have regretted not doing later? How did you feel? What about a time when you acted spontaneously or took a chance? Regardless of the outcome, how did you feel? Empowered?

List whatever comes to mind in the following space:

Chapter Summary

Live your life with no regrets. Seize the opportunities as they come.

Make your life one of action, and joy. Don't sit on the sidelines, hoping that maybe someday...

Chapter Sixteen: Friends First

Friendship is one of the great joys of our lives. Our friends share our experiences and in this sharing make those experiences richer. Surely you want the person who shares physically, mentally, and emotionally the majority of your life to be a friend, your best friend hopefully!

Frequently, if a person is looking for someone to share her life with, she may rush into a relationship without carefully looking first. She meets someone who appears to be the right fit and immediately latches on. This takes many forms, such as over whelming him with expectations and invitations or becoming lovers before a friendship develops. These put unnecessary strains on a new relationship. Making love with someone you really don't know or may not really care for is not very gratifying. Making love with a person whose presence fills you with joy is.

What if after becoming friends you realize that the chemistry isn't there? This can give you the chance to turn a potential disaster into a friendship and chances are that person has friends to introduce you to. This is not as easy with someone you have placed large expectations on or immediately developed a physical relationship with. In hindsight, you may find that many of your relationships could have been more fulfilling if they had evolved strictly into friendships. As you grew to know that person, you would realized that as wonderful as he was, he was still not the person to be your lifelong partner. Any agony or pain you may have experienced in the realizing process could have been avoided. And you would still have a good friend, instead of an ex-whatever!

Probably the most important aspect of being friends is the shared activities you have to build your relationship on. You do not put the same expectations on a friend as you do a lover. So, if you are friends first, you have time to develop a genuine base of caring and then love.

Think back on relationships you have had in the past. Are there any you realize now could have been more beneficial if you had remained friends, instead of trying to create something else? Do you believe that friendship is important in a relationship, important enough to develop before you put great expectations on an other person? Does being lovers cloud your vision of the other person. You may want to take the following space to write down your feelings about what friendship really is. Also address its importance to you in a relationship. It may help to note past experiences that reflect this.

NOTES

Chapter Summary

Give yourself the opportunity to become friends before you rush into a sexual relationship. It will be worth the wait one way or another!

SECTION III

Introduction

The potential for perfection is within every relationship. It is up to you to uncover it and allow it to grow. In our relationships we get exactly what we believe we will. This has many different labels, the law of attraction, self-fulfilling prophecy, beliefs. Whatever you call it, it is a creation of our own making. When you enter into a relationship, the newness creates a magic around it, and the person sharing your life can do no wrong. As time goes by (the length of time is different for everyone, a week, month, year...), you may begin to notice things you hadn't seen before and "cute" traits aren't quite so cute anymore. You begin becoming uncomfortable with this person and your relationship.

What is happening here? Did you enter into a relationship with Jekyll and Hyde? Or, could you (and maybe your partner) be flavoring the relationship based on past experiences? What if you had been married before and you found out your husband was unfaithful. Would you bring that fear forward, afraid now to trust this new partner? If your husband of ten years would do that to you, how can you trust someone you've known only a year? Possibly you begin suspecting and accusing your partner of infidelities when there really haven't been any. Yet, if these actions on your part continue, he might assume the attitude of "Why not, I am already being accused of it anyway." Your fears then become a reality, and now the two of you have an even larger obstacle to overcome if the relationship is going to last.

Can you see how in this case the past was carried forward to taint something that wasn't tainted before?

Another problem of bringing the past forward is when you felt you were the person responsible for whatever wrongs there were. Your life could then be one in which you see in others what you think you did, because this is what you know. This process is called mirroring, and it is seeing in others what is inside of you. If you find yourself accusing someone of something or judging another for something, look inside to see if this isn't something you have hidden and need to release.

Leaving the past in the past can be difficult if you try to ignore it or avoid it. Leaving the past dead can be simple if you override it with positive emotions and habits and create an environment suitable to nourish and protect your relationship as it grows stronger and stronger.

This section gives suggestions for making the relationship you find one that brings joy to both of your lives.

The Potential For Perfection
Is Within Every Relationship

Chapter Seventeen: Dwelling On The Positive

Whatever you think about expands. If we continually dwell on negativity, fears, and uncertainty, they will be reflected in our lives. We will draw them to us because that is where the majority of our energy is existing. If we assume a positive attitude, expecting good to fill our life and expecting our experiences to be joyful, that is what we will see in our life. Anything outside of that will be dismissed as simply temporary. Do you dwell on the good traits, actions, and characteristics of your partner, rejoicing in them?

Do you complain to your friends about what your partner does that you feel is wrong? I would encourage you not to. By discussing with friends or acquaintances things you feel your partner has done "wrong" only gives strength to those appearances. Just as your discussing their wonderful qualities gives those qualities energy and life.

If you find yourself complaining about your partner to others, you might try the following. First, listen to what you are saying. If it is true or important to you, address this with your partner and clear the issue up. Secondly, ban yourself from complaining for a day, week, month. See if your relationship begins to improve along with your entire life.

A couple I know experienced their relationship falling apart rapidly. Each began resenting the other for actions and characteristics they took as personal affronts. After a year the relationship had digressed to the point where just being around them was unbearable. You could cut the hostility with a knife! Somehow, one day, one of them woke up and realized how far they had fallen from the original love they once shared.

The discussion was not easy. They both realized that so much anger and resentment had built up between them that resolving the issues seemed insurmountable. Together they arrived at a plan. Each one wrote down everything about the other that they disliked or found annoying and that created anger or resentment. Then, together they went to the plot of land they had originally planned as a garden (nothing had ever been planted; their energy had been on destruction). Together they dug a hole and each one tore what they had written into little pieces and buried it in the soil. Hand in hand, they went into their home.

Next, each one wrote on a clean sheet of paper every positive emotion that they could find or remember being in their partner. They then took these statements and hung them above their bed and then made love like they hadn't in more than a year.

They now understand the power of emotions and their own power to create whatever emotions they want. Their focus is on positive aspects of each other, leaving the negative dead and buried.

ACTION STEPS

List every quality you appreciate, love, and respect about your partner. Keep this where it is easily accessible. Write these qualities down as you are reminded of them throughout the days and nights. This will help to remind you of what your true feelings are when they are shadowed or forgotten.

I suggest that you work through these exercises together. By doing so, you strengthen your bonds to one another, thereby giving each of you the opportunity to see what you truly cherish in each other. The added bonus is now that you both know, you will find yourselves striving to fulfill each other's expectations.

Complete the following together:

Qualities I love about are:

I love it when you tell me:

Qualities I find endearing, charming, fun, sweet, and lovable about you are:

Some of the wonderful things you have done for me in the past are:

NOTES

Chapter Eighteen: Long-Term Outlook

Do you view your relationship as something fleeting and transitory, or do you see it as something you are committed to for the long run? If you have committed to your relationship, then live it. Nothing else makes much sense! Plan for the relationship five, ten and twenty years from now. You can do what it takes in the moment, to make it last for life, something that grows and expands with time.

There are few things in life that have steady, straight upward growth. Most investments, educations, diets, and relationships experience peaks, valleys, and plateaus. Understanding this gives you a strong hold from which to view your relationship. From this vantage point you will know if what is going on is just a brief upheaval in one of your lives or if it really is a downtrend. If it is a downtrend, face it and determine why it is happening and what can be done to reverse it.

The same goes for an ongoing plateau. We all have periods of complacency and nongrowth, but if your relationship begins stagnating and remains that way, you owe it to your commitment to each other to determine why this is happening and what can be done to resolve it!

An easy rut to get caught in is "who is right and who is wrong." Sometimes couples spend so much energy in fault finding and proving who is right that they lose sight of the fact that none of it matters in the long term. If you find yourselves trying to prove right and wrong, realize that as two individuals you will always have your own viewpoints and no amount of words or arguments will change these.

When you are committed to a relationship, the actions and information you need to resolve anything will come to you. This is because you believe in the relationship. The belief will draw to the two of you what you need most to succeed together.

When you are addressing a point of discomfort in your relationship, try doing so without negative tones or accusations. Remember, in a relationship it takes two people to create anything! Terminate the conversation when both of you feel the relationship is stronger.

If you are unable to break the pattern or reach a satisfactory conclusion together, seek outside help. There are many therapists and groups that cater exclusively to couples. If your relationship is committed to the long-term outlook, together you can do whatever it takes to maintain its growth and joy. Remember, look to the future, and hold hands in the present.

NOTES

Chapter Nineteen: Basis of Forever

RESPECT

One of the first things you must share is respect for each other. If you don't respect each other, how can you be equal partners? Why would you want someone in your life day in and day out if you didn't respect him? Respect is never looking down on someone, never wondering how that person could be so dumb, inept, silly. It is seeing your partner for what he is, different yet equal, an individual yet still a part of you.

How do you show respect for one another?

List the things each of you can do to increase your respect for each other. (Not what the other person can to to make you respect them more!)

ACCEPTANCE

It is doubtful that anyone can be exactly as you want him to be, some though are closer than others. It is helpful if you realize that even though there may be actions and attitudes your partner has that you do not agree with, they contribute to making that person the individual that he is. Accepting him exactly as he is gives you the opportunity to see him with clear vision, to see his brilliance. You will also see how spectacular you are for having attracted this person into your life!

List the traits you have the hardest time accepting about each other.

Now, what can each of you do yourself to accept these traits more readily?

LOVE

Love Is the glue that holds the universe together. It is the substance that we use to weave the beauty into our lives. Without love, what a sad world this would be. Love can make all things right again, making hearts smile when they never thought they would again. Love is the essential feeling, the knowing inside of you that having this person in your life makes your world a brighter place to be.

How do I love thee, let me count the ways ... List twenty actions you can do for each other to show your love.

JOY

Who can go through life without joy? Who wants to? If two people are truly for each other, supporting and uplifting, than joy must be an integral fiber of their relationship. It is the intimate jokes, laughter, and fun that make a relationship whole. This is what says the two of you are a team. This allows each of you to be as children and to be safe being that way.

Make it a habit to find something to laugh about or simply have fun with each day you spend together. How can you give each other permission to bring more enjoyment into your relationship?

TRUST

Trust is more than just knowing that your partner is faithful to you. It is complete faith. It is the knowledge that you always have someone to count on. Things are not always as they appear. If you have complete trust, you will know this and place total confidence in each other. It is also the inner knowledge that you keep commitments with each other and always have the support you need.

What are the qualities and actions you equate with trust?

How can you each be more trusting and trustworthy?

HONESTY

Honesty is telling the truth. It can be a feeling or something you have actually done or are going to do. If you hold on to it, or lie, it compounds itself. Many people are used to telling just enough to get what they want and holding back on the rest. Stress can stem from lack of honesty. The more honest you are, the more you open yourself up to love and creativity. Start your relationships off being completely honest. If you have nothing to hide from each other, your communications will flow more easily.

Are there any untruths that you need to air with your partner? (Don't worry about what they need to share with you. Just do what you need to do and this will open up the communication.)

If your partner tells you something that doesn't sound truthful, ask about it, and then believe what had been said.

COMMUNICATION

Communication is one of the most important parts of any relationship. Without communication, it is difficult for needs to be expressed, desires to be verbalized, and uncomfortable feelings to be brought to light. It is also virtually impossible to express your love, happiness, joy, and excitement without true communication. When issues, questions, differences, or desires arise, deal with them. You can confront them by bringing up whatever it is that is causing you discomfort. If you feel that your partner is uncomfortable about something, ask her about it in an open and accepting way. When listening to your partner, be as nonjudgmental as possible. And remember, often humor can lighten a tense situation. If you realize that in the long term a particular issue really has no relevance on your situation, it is okay to just let it go. Issues not dealt with stay under the surface and eventually build up resentments or anger. Communicate these feelings and get on with your lives. Don't let them fester when you know how much better dealing with them will make you feel!

Practice your communication with each other, being as open as you can possibly be.

You can also practice communication in your day-to-day world. State your feelings and needs in a constructive and nondemanding manner. See if this doesn't make you feel positive and happily in control of your life!

Chapter Twenty: Playing Together

Our society places emphasis on continual entertainment. As children our parents entertain us, as we grow up we find that 24-hours-a-day there are television, radio, movies, sports, whatever form of entertainment you desire. This affects our lives by creating a world constantly looking outward. Like spoiled young princesses in a palace, wee have jesters dancing everywhere.

Somewhere alone the line we may also have come to believe that when we are in a relationship it becomes our partner's responsibility to entertain us. Unfortunately, we may believe this and look to our mates for playing instructions. If they do not have a quick, ready-made solution to boredom, we become disappointed. Unhealthy words for a relationship are those that are used to describe a lack of excitement or enthusiasm. All of a sudden our dreams burst, and we realize that the person opposite us is not going to save us from boredom. No one can. We are 100 percent responsible for ourselves.

When a relationship starts lacking shared experiences and fun, one or both partners may go outside of the relationship for these emotions. This could spell the death of something that had wonderful potential, but just needed some communication and fine tuning.

Instead of reaching that point, you may need to learn to appreciate simply being together — no plans, no obligations, just enjoying each others company. Many of us live in a rather hectic and hurried world. By taking the time to stop and simply be, we provide ourselves with a center of balance and strength to work from.

The paradox here is that the more we can quietly enjoy each other without the necessity of planned activities, the easier it will become to create activities and plans together.

ACTION STEPS

Creating goals together gives you a basis of shared dreams, visions, and desires. These goals can be anything, material, mental, spiritual, and emotional. Include where you want to be financially and physically and ways the relationship can grow and expand. Also, add activities you want to share and time you want to spend together.

Expanding your world will make you both more well-rounded people. It will give you shared experiences to base your relationship on. In the process you will learn more about each other, and your appreciation will flourish.

Goal-setting has three basic steps: stating the goal, planning the steps, and carrying through with the action. Each step is important.

In step one, describe the goal in its basic and complete form. Make sure you have as much clarity as possible when stating the goal. Leave room for change in the areas you are not sure of.

Next, write down the steps required to achieve the goal. This can be identical to your action calendar. The difference is that now there are two people's ideas, feelings and desires to take into consideration. So, be sure that your action steps reflect this. Both of you need to take responsibility for the goal. If one of you assumes financial responsibility, the other may want to do the legwork or homework.

Once you have decided on the actions to take, follow through. Not doing so subtly takes power away from the relationship. If either of you have trouble keeping commitments, look how you can reverse the habit. This may be done simply by stating to each other that you agree to do something. It may take marking it on your calendar or making a monetary commitment. By knowing what works for you, you make sure that you both carry through on what you say you will.

Some questions you can address to help determine relationship directions are:

What are shared activities you enjoy, and how can you expand on these?

What activities do you enjoy individually? How can you share these in the relationship?

Define your relationship presently. How would you like it to change in the next year, five years, ten years? How would you like it to remain the same?

How can you integrate your personal goals into those of the relationship?

My partner and I keep a notebook. Whenever we think of something we would love to do, we jot it down. Later, we glance through the notebook for inspiration and ideas. If you have difficulty thinking of ideas and activities to share, try brainstorming together with the following questions:

What would you do if you were kids? What if you were grown-ups?What if you were a different race or nationality? What is a skill or game you have wanted to learn? What volunteer work can you do together? What new type of music, show, or dance could you enjoy? Try a different church or service together. Would improvements could you make to your lives? Have a day where one of you makes all the decisions and the other agrees and enjoys (be sure to turn it around next time)!

Set goals and playtime together, and follow through with them. You are not just committing to activities but to your relationship as well! Live your commitment!

Chapter Twenty-one: Relationship Credo

Turning to my dictionary, I locate the meaning of credo or creed. *To believe, belief, confidence, a formulation of epitome of principles or rules, opinions, and precepts formally expressed and seriously adhered to and maintained.* A combination whose first constituent means "magic power" and whose second constituent is the verb represented by do; to bring to pass or carry out.

I translate this:

Make a statement of belief and carry it through.

Recently I read Robert Fulghum's wonderful book All I Really Need to Know I Learned in Kindergarten. In it, he shared his own personal credo. My inner voice said to me "What a wonderful thing to have in a relationship! Together you can create your perfect existence! If ever a doubt arises, all you need to do is look upon what you have written together: the credo of your love."

In my heart, that is magic and truth. You state what and who you are together. What your love has created. You then declare it to the universe and live it. How could a relationship not work, given those circumstances?

What are marriage vows if not a relationship credo? Recently one of my best friends married a wonderful lady. To be in their presence is love, sunshine, and smiles. They understand living the vows they have made. In addition, they created "The twelve rules of marriage." The rules are written for their personal circumstance and for the life they want.

The central point is that they took the time to write the rules. Their rules are not restrictive; they are building blocks. Safety checks for their life together. By composing these rules they have said to each other: "This is how great our love is, we have created it to stay!" The one rule of theirs is the one that made me realize the enormity of marriage vows. Traveling is their favorite hobby, and so they knew they would be visiting other cultures. Every new country they visit, they plan on remarrying according to that custom. They will stand in front of whomever holds the marriage power, in whatever language, and repeat their vows. They will them hang each of these marriage certificates on their wall as a remembrance and reminder.

Bob Mandell, the author of Two Hearts Are Better Than One, writes about creating a joint implant. This is a declaration of the qualities in your relationship you wish to expand. His and his wife Mallie's rule is: whenever one partner begins to repeat this declaration, the other must join in. He also states that the implant should be long enough so that it is hard for any negative thoughts to hold on by the time you have completed saying it.

Their joint implant is: "Bob and Mallie now have and enjoy ever-increasing love, health, happiness, wealth, wisdom, harmony, full self-expression, luxurious living spaces, easy and pleasurable travels, and sexual bliss."

Another powerful yet simple declaration are the words I love you. Said with conviction, these words convey everything a relationship can be.

Marriage vows, to joint implants, rules of the relationship, and "I love you" are all methods of restating and acting upon your love and life together.

Remember, belief is tantamount to creation. With the belief that you can do and have whatever you want, nothing can stop you.

SUGGESTED READING LIST

Section I

Open Heart Therapy: Bob Mandel, Celestial Arts.
This is an excellent book designed to ferret out emotions and blocks that may be holding you back.

Bridge Across Forever: Richard Bach, Morrow
A wonderful love story. This is the story that opened me up to the wonderful possibilities a relationship can have.

You Can Heal Your Life: Louise Hay, Hay House Publishing
This book deals with healing not only your physical body (Ms. Hay healed herself of cancer) but your emotional self as well. It is an excellent metaphysical guide to understanding yourself.

How to Create Your Holy Relationship: Edwene Gaines, Prosperity Products, P.O. Box 294, Mentone, Al. 65984
This is a booklet available on a love-offering basis. Edwene created the relationship she desired through prayer and declaration. This is a nice guideline if you have a metaphysical/spiritual outlook.

Holy Relationship Affirmation Cards: Twenty-one statements of power to assist you in creating your divine partner. Also, one affirmation prayer to use daily. These are also available from Prosperity Products (see address above).

SECTION II:

Two Hearts Are Better Than One: Bob Mandel, Celestial Arts
Bob tells his story of meeting his wife, Mallie, and the specifics of creating their relationship. He includes his "Create A Mate" suggestions and workbook for fun and helpful reading.

Making Love Happen: Rebecca Syndor, British American Publishing
As the owner of Romance Management Company in San Francisco and director of Romance for Korbel Cellars, Rebecca is the perfect author for this women-only book. She has created a step-by-step guide to finding an appropriate mate by using your intelligence and a little old-fashioned manipulation!

Fifty Ways to Find a Lover: Sharon Wolf, Bob Adams, Inc.
Techniques and skills for meeting people. Written by a consultant who leads workshops under the same name. Informative, with good ideas.

Creative Visualization: Shakti Gawin, Bantam Book/New World Library
The best book ever written on the art of visualization. Shakti goes through all of the various processes of visualization and how to apply them to your life.

SECTION III:

How to Make Love All of The Time:
Dr. Barbara De Angelis, Dell
This book was inspired by the experiences of the thousands who have undergone personal transformation after attending Dr. De Angelis' Making Love Work Seminar. This is the best book I have read on relationships. I find it a tremendous source of knowledge and inspiration.

Heart Over Heels: Bob Mandel, Ten Speed Press
Bob takes a fictional relationship and applies the principals of his first two books to it. He also delves heavily into rebirthing and the role of the birth process plays in relationships.

LifeMates: H. Bloomfield, and S. Vettese, New American Library
Written from this couples own experience. The book offers easy-to-understand strategies, love fitness tests, and relationship workouts. It will inspire couples to stay together and create what they really want in each other.

MISCELLANEOUS:

Loving Relationship Training: 1-800-INTLLRT
For individuals or couples, call for a schedule and additional information.

Making Love Work Seminar: 213-820-6600
The original inspiration for Dr. De Angelis' book. The seminar takes place over a weekend, and is open to singles, couples and families interested in creating more love in their lives.

To order additional copies of Single Smart, send 14.95 (check or money order) for each book ordered.

If you would like information on seminars in your area or the upcoming Single Smart tape set, please send a S.A.S.E to: (include the metropolitan area(s) you live nearest to)

Calico Publishing
P.O. Box 276
Seabrook, Tx. 77586

ALL ORDERS UNCONDITIONALLY GUARANTEED!